C000143813

Hg2 | Dubai

A Hedonist's guide to…

Dubai

Hallie Campbell and
Collette Lyons

Managing director – Tremayne Carew Pole
Marketing director – Sara Townsend
Sales director – Ben Illis
Design – Nick Randall
Maps – Nick Randall
Repro – Advantage Digital Print
Printer – Leo Paper
Publisher – Filmer Ltd

Email – info@hg2.com
Website – www.hg2.com

Published in the United Kingdom in January 2010 by
Filmer Ltd
17 Shawfield Street
London SW3 4BA

All rights reserved. No part of this publication may be reproduced or transmitted in any form or by any means, electronic or mechanical, including photocopy, recording or any other information storage and retrieval system without prior permission in writing from the publisher.

ISBN – 978-1-905428-35-9

Hg2 Dubai

How to…

A Hedonist's guide to Dubai is broken down into easy to use sections: Sleep, Eat, Drink, Snack, Party, Culture, Shop, Play and Info. In each section you'll find detailed reviews and photographs. At the front of the book is an introduction to Dubai and an overview map, followed by introductions to the main areas and more detailed maps. On each of these maps the places we have featured are laid out by section, highlighted on the map with a symbol and a number. To find out about a particular place simply turn to the relevant section, where all entries are listed alphabetically. Alternatively, browse through a specific section (e.g. Eat) until you find a restaurant you like the look of. Surrounding your choice will be a coloured box – each colour refers to a particular area of the Dubai. Simply turn to the relevant map to find the location.

Book your hotel on Hg2.com

We believe that the key to a great Dubai break is choosing the right hotel. Our unique site now enables you to browse through our selection of hotels, using the interactive maps to give you a good feel for the area as well as the nearby restaurants, bars, sights, etc., before you book. Hg2 has formed partnerships with the hotels featured in our guide to bring them to readers at the lowest possible price. Our site now incorporates special offers from selected hotels, as well information on new openings.

The concept

A Hedonist's guide to Dubai is designed to appeal to quirky, urbane and the incredibly stylish traveller. The kind of person interested in viewing the city from a different angle – someone who feels the need to explore, shop and play away from the crowds of tourists and become part of one of the city's many scenes. We give you an insider's knowledge of Dubai; Hallie and Collette want to make you feel like an in-the-know local, and take you to the hottest places in town (both above and under ground) to rub shoulders with the scenesters and glitterati alike.

Work so often rules our life, and weekends away are few and far between; when we do manage to break away we want to have as much fun and to relax as much as possible with the minimum amount of stress. This guide is all about maximizing time. The photographs of every place we feature help you to make a quick choice and fit in with your own style.

Unlike many other nameless guidebooks we pride ourselves on our independence and our integrity. We eat in all the restaurants, drink in all the bars, and go wild in the nightclubs – all totally incognito. We charge no one for the privilege of appearing in the guide, and every place is reviewed and included at our discretion.

Cities are best enjoyed by soaking up the atmosphere: wander the streets, partake in some retail therapy, re-energize yourself with a massage and then get ready to revel in Dubai's nightlife until dawn.

Hg2 Dubai

Hallie Campbell

Hallie Campbell is an award-winning travel and lifestyle writer. She has lived in New York, Los Angeles, Tokyo and London. An indefatigable traveller, she got her first passport when she was four years old and never looked back. Her work has appeared in Condé Nast Traveller, House & Garden, Harper's Bazaar, The Week, and Prime Location, among others. She is also the author of DubaiChic, a guide to the best of Dubai. She first fell in love with Arabian culture watching Lawrence of Arabia at a film festival. Since then she has travelled throughout Egypt, Oman, Jordan, and the United Arab Emirates on assignments for a variety of publications. Hallie loves Dubai for its creative energy and crucial role as a positive force in the Middle East.

Collette Lyons

You might think that a budding travel writer would chose to spend a gap year collecting tie-die rugs and smug stories to bore fellow students with, but Collette's writing career started, age 18, at parenting title Junior magazine. A year spent writing about nurseries in Clapham and trying unsuccessfully to stop newborn babies peeing on Hermès cashmere was followed by a degree in History of Art and Theology from Cambridge, making her great value at a dinner party but essentially unemployable. Bitten by the travel bug, Collette traveled to Australia in 2005. A year in Sydney and a stint as a stylist's assistant later, she moved back to London where she worked on the Sunday Times Style and Happy Magazine, and freelanced for The Telegraph Magazine, Handbag.com, Swarovski Magazine, BMI Voyager and First. She is now based in Dubai, working as Deputy Editor of Grazia Middle East and trying to stay out of the sun.

Dubai

Dubai rises from the champagne coloured desert dunes like a shimmering mirage – there's an air of unreality, as if its gleaming towers and glittering palaces could float into the air, or back into the lamp of some hyperactive genie. It's a phenomenon: the first truly 21st century city, breathtaking in its modernity and creative energy, bursting onto the world stage and taking everyone by surprise. Just how did this dizzy desert upstart emerge out of the sands to captivate the world?

Dubai is the vision of the remarkable Al Maktoum dynasty – probably the most wildly successful ruling family in modern times. Their story begins in 1833, when Sheikh Maktoum bin Buti and around 800 followers moved from Abu Dhabi to set up trading in Dubai. At that time Dubai was a sleepy desert outpost perched on the banks of the Creek, where boats sailed up from the Arabian Gulf to sell their wares. The arrival of the Al Maktoums changed everything. Their drive, ambition, and business acumen transformed Dubai into a top trading port, attracting merchants from as far afield as India, Africa and Persia. Along with trade, Dubai's pearl industry flourished and was a major source of wealth until the invention of cultured pearls.

But Dubai's big moment came in 1966, when oil was discovered. The petrodollars poured in, but instead of squandering the cash on palatial palaces and fleets of Rolls Royces, the visionary Al Maktoum rulers invested in Dubai. They created a viable infrastructure and set long term goals for the city's development. Creating stability in the region was one of these goals. Working closely with former trade rivals Abu Dhabi and other Emirates, in 1971 the group decided to band together as one political entity, the United Arab Emirates. The policy has been a great success, enabling the region to prosper.

Because Dubai's oil supply was limited (unlike next door Abu Dhabi, whose oil reserves are vast), they needed other means of creating wealth to sustain growth. With its sunny climate, beautiful beaches and welcoming culture, tourism was an ideal choice, initially promoted by offering duty free shopping as an incentive. But Dubai needed a symbol of its desire to be one of the world's top travel destinations.

All great cities have a great hotel to represent it. In 1999 the Burj Al Arab was opened to huge acclaim. Its remarkable billowing sail structure and exceptional standards of luxury made it unique – so much so that it was billed as the 'world's only 7 star hotel'. Dubai had arrived.

Today Dubai stands as a symbol of stability and prosperity in the Middle East. It is also one of the world's most cosmopolitan cities: 80% of its population is expatriate, with people from more than 200 countries living and working together in pursuit of their dreams. As their dynamic ruler Sheikh Mohammed himself puts it, 'To dream of the future is one of the most beautiful things in life. We are not content only to dream, we also work hard, because our ambitions are great and so are our dreams.'

Dubai is also one of the world's fastest growing cities, so if you wonder why parts of town resemble a giant building site, here's why: in the next ten years Dubai plans to evolve into the greatest tourist destination on the planet, the financial power-house of the Middle East and an active presence on the world stage. The sheer scale of the projects is astounding, involving billions of dollars and the creative vision of some of the world's most talented designers, architects, futurists and entrepreneurs.

For visitors, Dubai is a master of seduction, with a genuine desire to please. Whatever your holiday fantasy, chances are you'll find it here, with hotels, dining, nightlife and shopping to rival the best anywhere. Dubai combines an ancient Arabic culture and history with the latest trends. In minutes you can travel from post-modern skyscrapers to timeless sand dunes, hip beach bars to Bedouin tents. Where else can you go snorkelling in the morning, ski down snowy slopes in the afternoon, enjoy a camel ride into the desert at sunset, then have a Michelin-starred meal in the evening, and dance 'til dawn to the hottest DJ at a nightclub? Dubai is an almost surreal experience. Like a story out of *1001 Nights*, her kaleidoscopic mix of experiences is an adrenaline rush to the senses.

SLEEP...

1. Al Maha
2. Desert Palm
3. The InterContinental
4. Jumeirah Bab Al Shams

EAT...

5. Al Hadheerah
6. Rare
7. Reflets par Pierre Gagniere

DRINK...

8. Belgian Beer Cafe
9. Eclipse

SNACK...

10. Bistro Madeleine
11. Central Perk
12. Epicure

PARTY...

13. Alpha
14. Plastik

CULTURE...

15. B21 Gallery
16. Jumana:
    Secret of the Desert
17. Third Line Gallery
18. Total Arts

SHOP...

19. Dubai Festiv
20. Outlet Mall

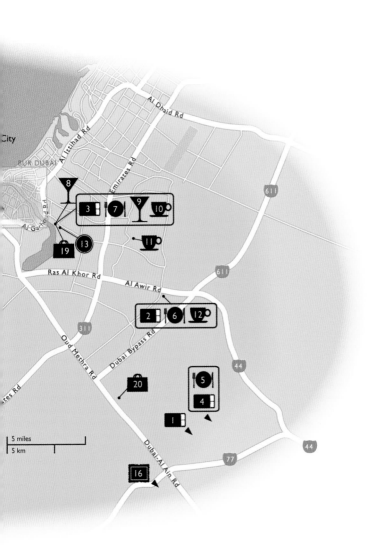

Dubai Overview

Bur Dubai, Deira & Festival City ◼

Bur Dubai

Bur Dubai was a sleepy desert outpost until the dynamic Al Maktoum clan arrived from Abu Dhabi eager to set up trade. In typical Al Maktoum fashion, they ended up running the place, attracting traders, merchants, and fortune-seekers.

Unlike the sleek, modern Dubai of Sheikh Zayed Road, Bur Dubai is crowded, congested and chaotic – all part of its charm if you're looking for a more real Dubai. This eclectic melting pot of Emirati, Indian, Pakistani, Iranian, Filipino and Sri Lankan cultures perfectly reflects Dubai's diversity. Where else in the world can you see a mosque, a Hindu temple, and a Sikh *gurudwara* all within a stone's throw of each other? These communities have been living in harmony for generations – all blending their talents to create today's Dubai.

One of the most influential of these early trading groups came from Bastak in Southern Iran, lured by the promise of tax-free concessions. The area along the Creek in Bur Dubai where they settled became known as 'Bastakiya' (see Culture) and many local families who are descended from the early settlers still live there. Happily, Bastakiya has been made a heritage preservation area – one of the very few places where you can wander about and get a feel for what life was like before the oil boom. Bastakiya's distinctive, century-old limestone and coral houses have high walls, intricately carved wooden doors and windows, wind towers to help cool the interiors with a flow of air, and gracious, shaded courtyards.

Stroll along the maze of winding lanes, now flourishing with chic galleries, like Majlis – a charmingly restored merchant's house with an excellent selection of pictures inspired by the region – and XVA, which exhibits the latest contemporary art and includes a guesthouse, shop and café. Visit the nearby historic Al Fahidi Fort, home to the Dubai Museum (see Culture), or enjoy a meal at one of Bastakiya's atmospheric restaurants, like Basta Art Café, Bastakiah Nights, or Local House, serving Emirati cuisine. It's best to go in the early evening, when the air cools and the evening lights come out and are reflected in the Creek.

Nearby you'll find the textile souks and ethnic cafes of Al Fahidi St. It's like stepping into a Bollywood stage set, a piece of India transported to the Gulf. Hindi film soundtracks blare out from streetside vendors, *sari*-clad women debate the silks on display, and the air is pungent with incense and the spices from simmering curries.

It's a maze of a place and very hot during the day, but in the evening it's fun and colourful, and a great place to find kitsch souvenirs like Mosque alarm clocks, sequined bellydancing outfits and singing toy camels – along with bargains on the latest gadgets.

For serious shoppers, head further afield to Karama, known for its copycat designer goods at knockdown prices. It may look slightly seedy, but as any seasoned Dubai bargain hunter will tell you, the tightly packed shops can't be beat for fab fake designer sunglasses, handbags, shoes and clothes, often so well done you really can't tell them from the real deal. Haggling is the order of the day, and a smile does wonders when you're hoping for that extra discount.

About a ten-minute stroll past the Bur Dubai Abra Station along the Creek brings you to the waterfront heritage area on Al-Shindagha Road. Here you'll find the beautifully restored Sheikh Saeed Al Maktoum House, and The Heritage and Diving Village (see Culture). Have a picnic in Creekside Park and watch the fascinating interplay of boats on the Creek, as ancient *dhows* sail past the yachts. The striking contrast between the gleaming steel skyscrapers and historic wind towers reflects Dubai's respect for the past in its pursuit of the future.

Deira

On the surface Deira looks run-down and somewhat shambolic, but once you get used to its jumbled atmosphere you'll find a genuine, thriving community far removed from the air-kissing crowd in Jumeirah. The best way to get to Deira is by *abra*, the traditional Dubai water taxi, from the Abra Station in Bur Dubai. Thousands of locals commute by *abra* and it's a great way to see the Creek. It's also the best deal in Dubai, at 1dhs, recently increased from 50 fils, which had been the price as long as anyone could remember. Just buy a ticket, join the jostling queue and hop on to the rickety-looking craft that awaits.

When you land at Deira you are perfectly positioned to explore the Spice Souk, one of the few traditional Arabian souks left out of the hundreds that used to flourish before the arrival of air-conditioned shopping malls put them out of business. Teeming with exotic characters that look like they could have wandered out of a Bedouin camp, the souk has a huge selection of dates and nuts as well as aromatic spices from the Middle East and India.

Nearby, the perfume souk is a seductive stop, as the perfumers blend essential oils like sandalwood and rose, vetiver and musk, to make the heady, distinctive perfumes favoured by Arabians. The scents come in distinctive glass vials and make excellent gifts.

Deira's most famous souk is the Gold Souk, capital of bling, where everything

that glitters is the real deal. Go at night to get the full atmosphere, as that's when the locals shop. Dubai is the worlds leading re-exporter of gold and prices are set by weight. You can negotiate depending on how much workmanship is involved – simpler pieces should always be cheaper. One of the special things about the Gold Souk is that you can get jewellery made up to your own design. Craftsmen are on site and can create a unique piece, usually in 24 hours or less.

Just behind the north end of the Gold Souk are two historic gems, Heritage House and Al Ahmadiya School (see Culture), both founded by one of Dubai's great merchant princes, Sheikh Mohammed bin Ahmed bin Dalmouk, who cornered the pearl trade.

Another glimpse into Dubai's past is at the *dhow* wharfage on the Creek at Bandi-yas Road, where you can still see these traditional trading vessels, some a century old, unloading their wares – although these days, the cargo is more likely to be computers than rare silks. Along the Creek, you'll find such Dubai landmarks as the towering blue glass triangle of the Dubai Chamber of Commerce & Industry, the sloping tablet of the National Bank of Dubai, which turns to a golden ingot in the light of the setting sun, and the Dubai Creek Golf & Yacht Club, whose soaring white roofs were designed to resemble the sails of a traditional Arab *dhow*. There are palaces and warehouses, fishing boats and floating warehouses, mega-yachts and rusty trawlers – all adding to the buzz that makes the Creek waterfront one of the most enjoyable places to wander about in Dubai.

Festival City

The eastern section of the Creek, just over Garhoud Bridge, is getting a massive makeover with the launch of Dubai Festival City, an ambitious multi-billion dollar project to completely revitalise the waterfront. Although the development is still under construction, there are enough venues open to make it well worth a visit. There are 4 kms of scenic Creekside views, with walkways, canals, fountains, restaurants and the latest designer boutiques, as well as a marina and a lively boating scene.

The Festival Promenade has panoramic views over Festival Marina and Dubai Creek, and links the InterContinental Hotel and Crowne Plaza with the Festival Centre shopping mall, which won the award for International Shopping Centre of the Year at the 2008 Global Retail and Leisure International Awards. DFC (as the locals call it) has so much going on, it's more of a lifestyle centre than a place to shop, and has become a favourite hangout for Dubai's trendy retail warriors. When complete, DFC will cover an area of 2.1 million square feet, with 550 shops, a 12-screen cinema complex, bowling centre and 90 international restaurants, including 40 *al fresco* dining venues along Canal Walk.

New hotels like are adding their glamour to the new neighbourhood, such as the five-star InterContinental, whose 35-floors have dramatic views over the Creek. Nearby, the new 18-hole championship Four Seasons Golf Club is already a landmark, with its dramatic, modernist clubhouse based on the arc of a golfer's swing, and the completion of the Four Seasons luxury resort hotel is keenly anticipated. With so much happening in this part of town, Dubai Festival City promises to be the most exciting new development on the Creek.

Bur Dubai, Deira, Festival City

SLEEP...

1. Grand Hyatt Dubai
2. Hilton Dubai Creek
3. Orient Guest House
4. Raffles Dubai
5. XVA Art Hotel

EAT...

6. Aangan
7. Bastakiah Nights
8. Bateaux Dubai
9. Fire & Ice
10. Lemongrass
11. Manhattan Grill
12. The Noble House
13. Persia Persia
14. Il Rustico
15. Shabestan
16. Sushi Sushi
17. Thai Kitchen
18. Verre

DRINK...

19. The Cellar
20. Crossroads
21. Ginseng
22. Rock Bottom
23. The Terrace

SNACK...

24. Al Mallah
25. Bait al Wakeel
26. Basta Art Café
27. The Boardwalk
28. Fish Basket
29. Organic Food & Café
30. Ravi
31. Wafi Gourmet
32. XVA Gallery Café

2000ft
1 km

PARTY...

33. Chi at the Lodge
34. China Moon
35. Irish Village
36. Maharlika Café Filipino
37. Plan B
38. Submarine
39. Warehouse

SHOP...

48. Burjuman
49. Gold Souk
50. Karama
51. Wafi City Mall

CULTURE...

40. Al Ahmadiya School
41. Dubai Museum
42. Heritage & Diving Village
43. Heritage House
44. Khan Murjan Gallery
45. Majlis Gallery
46. Sheikh Mohammed Centre
    Sheikh Saeed Al
47. Maktoum House
48. XVA Gallery

Jumeirah & Dubai Marina

This beachfront playground is where the action is, home to many of Dubai's rich and famous, and a favourite destination for visitors. In general, the area known collectively as Jumeirah meanders along the coast between Port Rashid and Dubai Marina, taking in the upscale neighbourhoods of Al Sufouh and Umm Suqeim. Along its immaculate, palm-fringed boulevards you'll find fabulous villas, five-star resorts, chic shopping enclaves and mega-bucks developments, like the newly opened Palm Jumeirah, a man-made island in the shape of a palm frond, home to Dubai's newest resort, the wonderfully over-the-top Atlantis. Best of all, you'll find the beach.

One of the great pleasures of Jumeirah is being on the water. The Arabian Gulf is warm and clear, a delight to swim in and perfect for every kind of water sport. It's also a beautiful stretch of water, turning from aquamarine to deep sapphire during the day, and reflecting the moon in a radiant shimmer at night. The beaches along Jumeirah are tranquil and inviting, with the Jumeirah Beach Park one of the best public beaches – Dhs 5 for admission, but worth it for the facilities. It has a long stretch of sand, changing rooms, showers, lifeguards on duty, a children's play area and a lawn with shady trees – ideal for a picnic. If your hotel doesn't have a big beach to play on, this is a great alternative to sitting at a crowded pool. Nearby Safa Park is also a pleasant place to relax and people-watch.

Jumeirah is home to Dubai's best resorts, including the breathtaking Burj Al Arab. Next-door is the futuristic, wave shaped Jumeirah Beach Hotel (and its exciting Wild Wadi waterpark), the Ritz Carlton, One&Only Royal Mirage and the Madinat Jumeirah resort among others. With so many top hotels, Jumeirah nightlife is excellent – venues like the Kasbah at One&Only Royal Mirage and Jam Base at Madinat Souk attract a party crowd until way after midnight.

With all that money floating around, it's no surprise that Jumeirah has some of the best shopping in Dubai. Mall of the Emirates is one of the world's great retail emporiums. Within its massive interior are literally hundreds of shops, from Accessorize to Zara. It's also one of Dubai's most famous places to hang out, with a myriad variety of places to eat and drink, the unmissable Ski Dubai, a Cineplex cinema and Magic Planet indoor amusement arcade.

Nearby, Souk Madinat is an Arabian-style bazaar, with boutiques, galleries, artisans at work, and a stylish, sophisticated array of restaurants, bars and entertainment centres. It's magical at night – with its soaring architecture: wind towers, bridges, roof terraces, courtyards and a scenic waterway lit by hundreds of lanterns, with small *abra* water taxis ferrying people into the Madinat Jumeirah resort.

The Mercato Mall on Jumeirah Beach Road is a gem of Dubai Italianate kitsch, built to resemble a Venetian piazza, and very popular with locals who come in to top up at Topshop, check out the latest videos from the Virgin Megastore and buy pastries at Paul. Café society is all the rage, and not just Starbucks: Lime Tree Café, Second Cup and Fudo are all local hot spots, as Jumeirah's social butterflies flit to coffee houses and cafés to exchange the latest gossip while checking out each other's designer wardrobes.

The Jumeirah coast is so popular that new developments are rapidly changing the scene. As if The Palm and The World manmade offshore islands weren't enough, Dubai's insatiable demand for housing has made constant construction an ongoing part of life. Not long ago Dubai Marina (www.dubaimarina.ae) was just a building site; now it's at the epicentre of what's being called ' New Dubai'. The graceful waterway, lined with aristocratic yachts, winds its way past Grosvenor House, one of Dubai's most stylish hotels, and the Buddha Bar, an oriental fantasy restaurant and nightclub, along the newly fashionable Marina Walk. This pedestrian-friendly promenade is fast filling up with chic boutiques, outdoor cafés and restaurants like new seafood star Blue, retro burger bar Johnny Rockets, and the glamorous new Dubai Marina Yacht Club.

Lining the waterway are the glittering towers of Jumeirah Beach Residences, ('JBR' to locals) a luxury residential development billing itself as 'the lifestyle of a lifetime' and the largest single-phase residential development in the world. Nearing the final stage of completion, it will feature 36 residential towers, four hotels with four beach clubs, a beach park and The Walk, a seriously swanky mall with ultra hip shops, like Boutique 1, already open for business. The development has gobbled up most of Jumeirah's remaining beachfront – much to the annoyance of long-term residents, who have to deal with ever-dwindling beach access. Other developments part of 'New Dubai' are Media City, home to many top communications companies like Reuters, and Knowledge City, a high tech enclave that's an IT geek's dream come true.

In Jumeirah, the beautiful people meet and mingle under starry skies and serene seas, enjoying the quintessential Dubai mix of sun, fun and style. For many locals and visitors, Jumeirah is what the good life is all about. Strolling along the beach at sunset, with the sky an iridescent glow, the Burj Al Arab gleaming in the distance, and a gentle breeze coming in off the Gulf, it's easy to see why.

Jumeirah, Dubai Marina

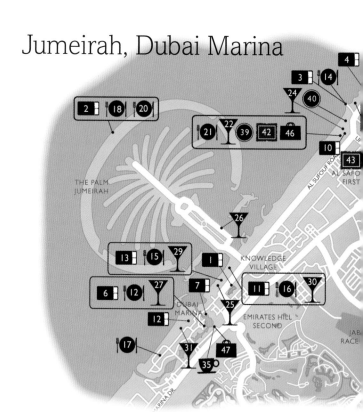

🖼 SLEEP...

1. Arjaan
2. Atlantis
3. Burj al Arab
4. Fusion I & II
5. Fusion Boudoir Apartments
6. Grosvenor House
7. Harbour Hotel & Residences
8. Jumeirah Beach Hotel
9. Kempinski Hotel
10. Malakiya Villas
11. One & Only Royal Mirage
12. Le Royal Meridien
13. Westin Dubai

🍽 EAT...

14. Al Mahara
15. Bussola
16. Eau Zone
17. Frankie's
18. Nobu
19. Rhodes Mezzanine
20. Ronda Locatelli
21. Segreto

🍸 DRINK...

22. The Agency
23. Après
24. Bahri Bar
25. Barasti
26. Bidi Bondi
27. Buddha Bar
28. Mosaic Chill
29. Oeno
30. The Rooftop
31. Trader Vic's
32. Uptown Bar

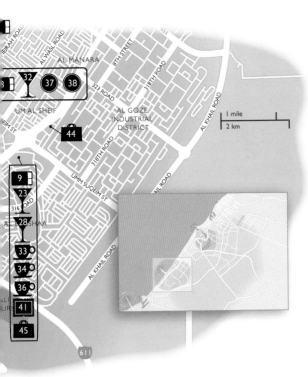

☕ SNACK...

33. Almaz by Momo
34. Emporio Armani Caffè
35. Johnny Rockets
36. Sezzam

◼ CULTURE...

41. DUCTAC
42. Madinat Theatre
43. Meem Gallery

👜 SHOP...

44. Gold & Diamond Park
45. Mall of the Emirates
46. Souk Madinat
47. The Walk

● PARTY...

37. 360°
38. The Apartment
39. Jambase
40. Soluna

Downtown Dubai

Along Sheikh Zayed Road, between Interchange 1 and the new Burj Dubai Interchange, a phalanx of mighty skyscrapers heralds the epicentre of Dubai's economic miracle. Downtown is where the money gets made, the deals get done and Dubai's future is planned. Here, you'll find five-star hotels like Jumeirah Emirates Towers, The Fairmont, and Shangri-La, as well as gleaming shopping malls like the designer-only Boulevard. There's also the Dubai International Finance Centre and the fledgling DIFX stock exchange, based at The Gate, an imposing steel and glass archway also home to The Gate Village, a newly developed area now bustling with galleries, stylish shops and cafés. From 9am to 5pm, Downtown buzzes like a hyperactive hive, but once the sun goes down and the neon lights up, the atmosphere switches to party mode: Downtown has a large share of Dubai's favourite watering holes. (See Drink & Party) where you can see the city's players in action.

Dubai's downtown is heading for a radical change with the arrival of Burj Dubai, the much-hyped tallest building in the world, and the symbol of Dubai's fearless optimism and creative flair. Around its swirling towers, an entire community is being created, called Downtown Burj Dubai. This 1km business, retail, and residential district will expand outwards from the extraordinary Burj, adding a dynamic new element to the downtown scene.

At its heart, the tower itself is a feat of both engineering and aesthetics. Inspired by the grace of the Hymenocallis flower, which blooms in the region, and traditional Islamic architecture, its fascinating design, by award-winning architect Adrian Smith, is being hailed as a modern masterpiece. For Dubaians, it is more than an amazing new building; it is a statement of their arrival on the world stage.

Inside Burj Dubai will be restaurants, elite shops, residential apartments, businesses, a stunning observation lounge on the 124th floor, and the world's first Armani Hotel, bearing Giorgio Armani's signature style of simple elegance – achieved at great expense. Armani is also in charge of creating the interiors for the residential apartments, including a penthouse tipped to be the most expensive ever.

Just across from the tower, the Burj Dubai Lake has been created where there was once just sand. In the middle is 'Old Town Island' (although ironically brand new), which will feature an attractive residential area with market squares, waterfront restaurants and traditional Arabian architecture – along with Souk Al Bahar, a series of shops in a picturesque arcade showcasing Dubai's cultural heritage. The new five-star Palace Hotel, designed to reflect the beauty of classical Arabian architecture, and The Address, a hip hotel with one of the best outdoor terraces in town, is already attracting a glamorous crowd. There's also Burj Dubai Square, an outdoor pedestrian shopping and leisure area, and in keeping with Dubai's love of superlatives, the world's biggest retail complex, Dubai Mall.

When Dubai Mall opened, Downtown virtually ground to a halt as thousands flocked to see this capital of consumerism in action. Imagine 1,200 stores, including the world's largest gold souk, a separate Fashion Island with 70 designer boutiques dedicated to haute couture, one of the world's largest aquariums; an Olympic-sized ice skating rink; the region's first SEGA indoor theme park and The Grove, an indoor-outdoor streetscape with a fully retractable roof. Even by Dubai standards it's an impressive, excessive adventure in retail heaven – a place where you can literally shop 'til you drop.

Downtown Dubai

SLEEP...

1. The Address
2. Fairmount Dubai
3. Jumeirah Emirates Towers
4. La Maison d'Hotes
5. The Palace

EAT...

6. Asado
7. Empire
8. Momotaro
9. Okku
10. Rivington Grill
11. Smiling BKK
12. Teatro
13. Zuma

DRINK...

14. Cin-Cin
15. Harry's Ghatto
16. iKandy Ultra Lounge
17. Left Bank
18. Neo's
19. Sho Cho
20. Vu's

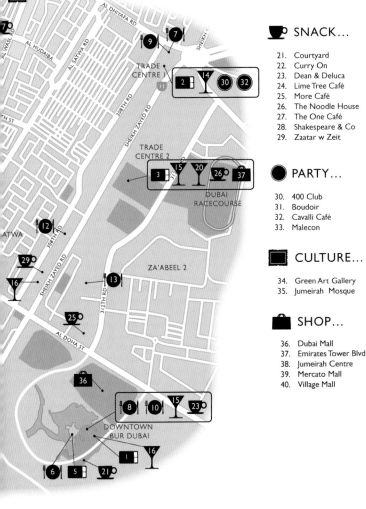

SNACK...

21. Courtyard
22. Curry On
23. Dean & Deluca
24. Lime Tree Café
25. More Café
26. The Noodle House
27. The One Café
28. Shakespeare & Co
29. Zaatar w Zeit

PARTY...

30. 400 Club
31. Boudoir
32. Cavalli Café
33. Malecon

CULTURE...

34. Green Art Gallery
35. Jumeirah Mosque

SHOP...

36. Dubai Mall
37. Emirates Tower Blvd
38. Jumeirah Centre
39. Mercato Mall
40. Village Mall

sleep...

Whether it's a simple Bedouin tent under the stars or the £23,000 a night Bridge Suite at Atlantis, Dubai has a greater variety of places to stay than any other city its size on the planet. So whatever your fantasy, the chances are Dubai will have the hotel to match. You'll find beachfront blissouts, high city style, desert adventure, spa retreats, romantic escapes, a cosy b&b or palace fit for a sheikh – it's all here.

Dubai's rapid growth means it's more important than ever to plan where you want to stay, depending on the sort of holiday you're after. If you're longing to flop on a beach it makes no sense to book a hotel in Deira because you'll spend all your time in traffic. If hanging out in the souks and soaking up an Arabian atmosphere is more to your liking then you may not want to be in a beach resort in Jumeirah. And if you like nightlife, people and partying, a hotel out of town in Jebel Ali or the desert probably won't have the buzz you're after.

For sun, sand and surf stay on the coast in upscale Jumeirah, where most of the best resorts are located and there are a huge variety of activities to choose from. If you're bringing the family, the beach resorts with the best kids clubs are Jumeirah Beach Hotel, Madinat Jumeirah, Atlantis, Ritz-Carlton and One&Only Royal Mirage. Jumeirah is where everyone goes to relax and have fun, as popular with locals as it is for tourists.

For a more urbane, less touristy atmosphere stay in town or Dubai Marina. For sheer style and sophistication it's hard to beat Emirates Towers, Grosvenor House or Park Hyatt, while new areas like Downtown Burj Dubai, home of the world's tallest building, have exciting new hotels like The Address.

If a genuine Arabian experience and a feeling for culture and heritage is what you're after, spend a night or two in the desert at Al Maha or Bab Al Shams, or in Dubai's atmospheric Bastikiya at haute-bohemian XVA or charming Orient House.

If you want to get away from the crowds, but not too far from Dubai's fun zones, the new Desert Palm is a hedonist hideaway.

Some hotels are destinations in themselves. Burj Al Arab and Atlantis are as much about fantasy as a place to stay, while resorts like One&Only Royal Mirage and Madinat Jumeirah (left) are so perfectly conceived and orchestrated, you could spend your whole holiday without leaving the hotel and not regret it.

If your holiday dream includes spending quality time in a top spa, check out Talise Spa at Madinat Jumeirah, Amara at Park Hyatt, Retreat at Grosvenor House, Amrita at Raffles or the Spa at The Palace.

Shopping in Dubai is so good; some people come purely to fill their suitcases and some of the best shopping malls have hotels included: shop Wafi and stay at Raffles, Kempinski at Mall of Emirates, The Palace at Dubai Mall, Emirates Towers for The Boulevard, or the new InterContinental for Dubai Festival City.

Dubai's hotels are engaged in an ongoing turf battle for your heart and wallet. As a result, service and standards tend to be high across the board. However the increasing demand for staff as more hotels open has led to some criticism recently that new arrivals aren't as well trained as their predecessors.

Dubai's hotel scene is incredibly dynamic, with new hotels opening all the time. Highlights include the eagerly awaited Armani Hotel in Burj Dubai, the Palazzo Versace, the Four Seasons Dubai Festival City and the legendary ocean liner QE2, reincarnated as a luxurious floating hotel.

The rates listed are from the lowest priced room to the highest priced suite. Rates are quoted in AED (Arab Emirates Dirhams).

the best hotels

1. Burj Al Arab
2. Al Maha
3. Malakiya Villas
4. One&Only Royal Mirage
5. Grosvenor House
6. Ritz Carlton
7. Raffles
8. Park Hyatt
9. Atlantis
10. The Palace

1. Burj Al Arab
2. Grosvenor House
3. Park Hyatt
4. Desert Palm
5. The Address

1. Al Maha
2. One&Only Royal Mirage
3. Malakiya Villas
4. Bab Al Shams Desert Resort
5. Atlantis

Beach: Ritz Carlton
Desert: Al Maha Desert Resort & Spa
Downtown: Jumeirah Emirates Towers
Shopping: Kempinski Hotel Mall of the Emirates

The Address *(left)*
Burj Dubai Blvd.,
Downtown Burj Dubai
Tel: 04 436 8888
www.theaddress.com
Rates: AED 1,440–12,000

This innovative flagship from the new Address Hotels+Resorts caters to the modern 24/7 traveller offering 24-hour checkout, a 24-hour fitness centre and 24-hour restaurant dining. Located in the heart of Downtown Burj Dubai, The Address is next to the shopping opportunities of both the Souk Al Bahar and the new Dubai Mall, packed full of almost 1,200 shops. Inside the rooms are minimalist modern, with textured wood, glass and marble, kitted out with all the latest features like iPod docks and free WiFi. There is a cool kids club, and the exclusive spa features E'Spa treatments. The outdoor terrace is one of the best in town, with its five modernist tiered swimming pools, fountains, chill out zones in tented cabanas and wicker rocking lounges, with majestic views of Burj Dubai, the lyrical silver spiral that is the world's tallest building. Don't miss Neos (see Drink), the highest cocktail lounge in Dubai and seriously sophisticated, with its glittering black and chrome interior and hostesses in floor-length silver satin.

Style 7, Atmosphere 8, Location 8

Al Maha *(right)*
Desert resort and spa
Tel: 04 303 4222 www.al-maha.com
Rates: AED 4,230–7,100

This ultra chic desert eco-retreat is tucked into the billowing dunes of Dubai's largest conservation area – 225 sq kms of your own personal desert. Guests stay in seriously smart private pool villas with tented rooftops. Everything in the suites is arranged to make a stay at Al Maha as pleasurable as possible, from the the Bvlgari toiletries to the thoughtful field binoculars provided for you to examine the glorious desert wildlife outside your door. The resort has won nearly a dozen major awards since opening. Al Maha brilliantly mixes traditional Arabian style with European luxury – you can ride camels into the dunes one moment and have a facial at the blissful Timeless Spa the next. Activities include dune bashing in 4x4 jeeps, learning about the art of falconry, or riding Arabian horses at dawn through the desert, while nimble gazelles and desert Oryx race past. Children aren't allowed, which creates an atmosphere suited to relaxation and romance. Seductive evenings begin as the sun sets behind the champagne coloured dunes and millions of stars emerge across the desert sky.

Style 9, Atmosphere 9, Location 9

Atlantis *(bottom)*
Crescent Road, Palm Jumeirah
Tel: 04 426 0000
www.atlantisthepalm.com
Rates: AED 1,650 – 128,600

Atlantis, the new all-singing, all-dancing $1.5 billion, 1,539 room mega-resort by legendary hotelier Sol Kerzner, is a celebration of all things aquatic, featuring Aquaventure, a dynamic water park set in a tropical garden;

Ambassador Lagoon, a marine habitat including sharks and rays; and Dolphin Bay, where guests can meet and mingle with the dolphins. Atlantis is a theatrical extravaganza, with the marine theme echoed throughout the visually stunning resort. There's a cosmopolitan buzz: Russian oil barons make deals on their mobiles at the pool, in the lobby Sheikhs and their entourages sweep past in flowing robes, while chic euro yummy mummies watch their designer-clad offspring at the beach. It's brilliant for people watching. A far cry from understated, the resort's 'nothing succeeds like excess' mantra extends to dining, with four of the world's top chefs – Nobu Matsuhisa, Giorgio Locatelli, Michel Rostang and Spanish sensation Santi Santamaria, each creating their own themed restaurants. Add to that the jewel-like spa, state-of-the-art kid and teen zones, high-octane nightclub, pristine private beach, and delightful rooms with panoramic views of the Gulf. It's easy to see why Atlan-

tis is one of the most exciting places to stay in Dubai.

Style 9, Atmosphere 9, Location 6

....

Burj Al Arab *(above)*
Umm Suqeim, Jumeirah
Tel: 04 301 7777 www.jumeirah.com
Rates: AED 9,000–55,000

If Marilyn Monroe came back as a hotel, she'd be the Burj Al Arab: curvy, colourful, sexy and iconic, with an over-the-top style all of its own. Pop idols, movie stars, society scions, heads of corporations and heads of state have fallen under its spell. Rising in solitary splendour from its own private island like a magical vessel, the illuminated billowing sail is a symbol of Dubai's creative energy. The dazzling suites expand over two floors, linked by a marble spiral staircase perfect for making an entrance. Floor to ceiling windows overlook the sparkling Gulf, and high-

tech touch pads control everything from the a/c to the curtains. You'll find boudoir bathrooms, a personal laptop with WiFi, and huge beds with the softest linens. The butlers are among the best, happily catering to the whims of their guests. It's all about luxury, from the full-size Hermès toiletries to the Evian water sprays keeping you cool at the pool. Though you may never want to leave your suite, the hotel tempts you with such diversions as shopping trips in a Phantom Rolls Royce and helicopter jaunts from the hotel's own landing pad, and the exquisite Assawan Spa offers indulgent treatments (try the La Prairie caviar facial). Having drinks at the pricey but unmissable Skyview Bar, with its retro-chic disco style and bird's eye views, is a Dubai rite of passage.

Style 9, Atmosphere 9, Location 9

Desert Palm *(above)*
Al Awir Road, Dubai

Tel: 04 323 8888 www.desertpalm.ae
Rates: AED 1,587–24,343

New and already getting rave reviews for its departure from the usual Dubai five-star, Desert Palm is a true original. Just 15 minutes from the airport, this boutique retreat resides within 150 acres of gardens and polo fields of a private estate, reminiscent of an exclusive country club. For those looking for a total chillout with quiet privacy, exceptional cuisine, caring staff, a superb organic spa and stunning suites and pool villas, then Desert Palm is perfect. No stone is left unturned with pre-programmed iPods (7,000 songs to choose from), espresso makers, dvd players and a 'maxi bar'. The atmosphere is serene and relaxed – guests can watch the polo chukkas, stroll through the palm groves, laze in the huge swimming pool that runs the length of the terrace, enjoy the treatments of the Lime Spa, or linger over a delicious breakfast cooked to order (not a buffet in sight). What really sets Desert Palm apart is its attitude. There's a quiet attention to detail resonating throughout, with guests receiving exceptionally high levels of personal service. From the moment you walk in you are treated like a special friend and indulged accordingly.

Style 9, Atmosphere 8, Location 6

 **The Fairmont Dubai** *(top)*
Sheikh Zayed Road
Tel: 04 332 5555 www.fairmont.com
Rates: AED 1,099–33,000

The Fairmont is the quintessential Dubai hotel – sleek, sophisticated, and with an impressive battalion of facilities to please its well-heeled guests. Located in the heart of downtown, on Sheikh Zayed Road near the Trade Centre, you can get to most of Dubai's sights within a 10-15 minute taxi ride. The Fairmont is where Dubai's movers and shakers gather for a drink at Cin Cin or dinner at the Exchange Grill. The Friday Champagne Brunch at Spectrum On One is one of the best in Dubai, with free-flowing Moët & Chandon,. For chilling out, head for the stunning rooftop pools, while spa connoisseurs will enjoy the Willow Tree Spa. For some late night excitement, get on the guest list for the 400 Club, where Dubai's social butterflies are found dancing in their designer-wear best. The Fairmont is a high-powered hotel that consistently delivers, a good choice for those seeking glamour without glitz.

Style 8, Atmosphere 8, Location 7

 Fusion I & II *(bottom)*
off Al Wasl Road,
(between Safa Park & Jumeirah Beach Hotel) Jumeirah
Tel: 050 478 7539
www.fusionhotels.com
Rates: AED 550–750

Fusion is a new hip and happening boutique hotel group in Jumeirah, occupying two spacious villas and a selection of chic apartments in the sought-after Jumeirah Beach Residences. Think 'Wallpaper* goes to Dubai' and you get the idea. Thursday night barbecue parties attracts a glam crowd of Jumeirah's creative movers and shakers, a place where you can run into graphic designers, fashion models in town for a shoot, or entrepreneurs looking for their pot of gold. The atmosphere is friendly and laid-back, although some say too casual when it comes to confirming bookings and giving directions to its hard to find locations. All the rooms are decorated with great flair and individuality. Breakfast at the huge communal table is especially popular for networking and nursing hangovers. Fusion best suits independent singles or friends travelling together – it's too social for loved up couples who want privacy and too offbeat for traditionalists who want things like 24-hour room service. If you want a funky space at an unbeatable price, Fusion is one of Dubai's unique places to stay. Just go with the flow.

Style 8, Atmosphere 7, Location 6

Grand Hyatt Dubai *(top)*
Umm Hurair
Tel: 04 317 1234
dubai.grand.hyatt.com
Rates: AED 1,400–2,100

The futuristic blue building spells 'Dubai' in Arabic. That's just one of the fun facts about this popular Dubai landmark near Garhoud Bridge. The hotel is famous for its full-sized Arabian *dhows* suspended from the ceiling, below them an indoor tropical garden interior on two floors, complete with running streams and little bridges, cascading flowers and towering palms. There is nothing else like it in Dubai. Unlike many business hotels, which can have a sterile, corporate atmosphere, the Grand Hyatt radiates warmth and flair. Service is caring and personal, a real achievement given it has more than 600 rooms and is always busy. It feels more like a resort than a city hotel, with a range of activities including squash, tennis, a 450m jogging track, indoor and outdoor pools, a full-on fitness centre, and the excellent Grand Spa. The highlight of hotel is its spectacular 37 acres of landscaped gardens and 3 huge freeform pools, among the biggest in Dubai. There are an impressive 14 restaurants and bars within the hotel. At the Grand Hyatt, big somehow manages to be beautiful.

Style 7, Atmosphere 8, Location 6

Grosvenor House *(left)*
Dubai Marina
Tel: 04 399 8888
www.grosvenorhouse-dubai.com
Rates: AED 2,500–7,000

Grosvenor House burst onto the scene a few years and became an instant classic, winning awards and single-handedly putting Dubai Marina on the map as a hangout for Dubai's bright young things. Glamorous and cutting edge, yet creative and unpretentious, GH is a masterpiece of design savvy and intuitive hotel service. It's also home to some of Dubai's favourite venues, with the fabulous Buddha Bar, chic Bar 44, (named after the 44 champagnes it serves) and Michelin-starred chef Gary Rhodes Mezzanine restaurant attracting a stellar crowd. Hedonists on holiday will find many pleasures, like Retreat, an entire floor devoted to sybaritic spa treatments, beauty, and fitness. The exceptionally comfortable bedrooms come with a butler and are cleverly designed to maximise light and space, with picture window views of mega-yachts lolling in the marina below. Construction is still going on at the Marina, so check when you book that your room is away from any current building works. All Grosvenor House lacks is a beach, but guests have complimentary access to its beachfront sister hotel, Le Royal Méridien Beach Resort & Spa. Good for business and even better for pleasure, GH is one of Dubai's top hotels and deservedly so.

Style 9, Atmosphere 9, Location 8

Hilton Dubai Creek *(right)*
Beniyas Road, Deira
Tel: 04 227 1111 www.hilton.com
Rates: AED 950–2,225

Not your average Hilton. Design junkies

will love this minimalist masterpiece of glass, wood and chrome by renowned architect Carlos Ott. The lobby, with its distinctive double staircase, is a Dubai landmark. The elegant guestrooms are ultra-modern, with clean lines and sleek furnishings and floor-to-ceiling windows with bird's eye views of the Creek. The chic black & white bathrooms are a plus. The hotel is home to Verre, Gordon Ramsay's only restaurant in Dubai and considered the best for gourmet French cuisine and serious wines. Deira is old Dubai, atmospheric if chaotic. Wander through the spice and gold souks where trading still goes on as it has for generations.

**Style 10, Atmosphere 7,
Location 5**

....

The InterContinental *(above)*
Dubai Festival City
Tel 04 701 1111

www.intercontinental.com
Rates: AED 1,500–8,220

When it opened last year, the Inter-Continental put the new Dubai Festival City development on the map as a place to visit. What was once a backwater is now a thriving shopping and entertainment destination. The depth of style of the new InterCon offering comes as a bit of a surprise, with far more attention to cutting-edge detail than normally associated with the brand. Bedrooms are big, bright and well designed, with sleek modern bathrooms. Highlights of the hotel include a beautiful pool area, the fab French restaurant Reflets by Michelin-starred chef Pierre Gagnaire, and the Vista Lounge, a popular cocktail bar that lives up to its name with panoramic views of the Creek. The hotel's award-winning concierge staff have excellent local knowledge, so don't hesitate to ask their advice. At Dubai Festival City

you can catch the latest concert, shop till you drop at the mall, or just stroll along the waterfront and watch the *dhows* laden with cargo come up the Creek as they have for centuries.

Style 7, Atmosphere 7, Location 6

Jumeirah Bab Al Shams Desert Spa & Resort *(above)*
Tel: 04 832 6699
www.jumeirahbabalshams.com
Rates: AED 2,100–7,300

Get in touch with your inner Lawrence of Arabia at this desert escape an hour's drive from Dubai. Bab Al Shams (Gateway to the Sun) is designed like a Bedouin fort, and blends seamlessly into the surrounding desert. Decorated in genuinely traditional Gulf style the 115 rooms are home to natural stone, dark wood, Arabian antique glasswork and textiles. The highlight of the ho-

tel is the pool, a massive 1,400 square metres expanse with sweeping views across the desert. When the sun dips behind the dunes, head up to the Al Sarab Rooftop Bar for cocktails as the dying light illuminates the desert in wonderful hues. The Al Hadheerah restaurant is open to the stars and in true, but slightly kitsch, 1,001 Nights style features a pantheon of camels, falcons, whirling belly dancers, musicians, and a small tented souk selling local crafts. Tuck into a pan-Arabic feast served from open cooking stations featuring wood-fired ovens, charcoal grills, and spit roasts. The real reason to stay out here is to experience the desert, from 4-wheel drives to horse and camel safaris.

Style 8, Atmosphere 7, Location 9

Jumeirah Beach Hotel *(left)*
Jumeirah Beach Road
Tel: 04 348 0000 www.jumeirah.com
Rates: AED 3,200–9.600

Rising above Jumeirah's coastline like a surreal metallic wave, the Jumeirah Beach Hotel is a well-loved landmark that holds its own against all the newcomers. For watersports it is probably the best resort in Dubai. The hotel's Pavilion Dive Centre has been accredited as as both a Padi 5 Star Gold Palm IDC resort and National Geographic Dive Centre. If you want peace and quiet this is not the place. The resort is always busy, full of people, all out for a good time and getting it at such popular watering holes as The Apartment and Uptown Bar. By day collapse by the pool or beach or take advantage of free admission to Wild Wadi Waterpark next door – a sure way to get rid of any hangover. Clear your head after a late night

Style 6, Atmosphere 7, Location 8

Jumeirah Emirates Towers
Sheikh Zayed Road   *(right)*
Tel: 04 330 0000 www.jumeirah.com
Rates: AED 2,100–7,300

Located in the heart of the financial district, this sleek and sophisticated hotel is famous for its flawless service, state-of-the-art business facilities and favourite Dubai watering holes like Vu's bar, with its sky high views of the city, Scarlett's for casual dining and a lively bar scene, and the much-loved Noodle House, where even Sheikh Mohammed pops in for a bite. The hotel's Shopping Boulevard is one of the most exclusive in Dubai. Rooms are modernist, understated bling-free zones in soothing neutral tones, with plenty of space to work or relax. H2O The Spa for Men is where Dubai's high flying execs go for stress relief in the form of soothing treatments. Although primarily a top business venue, Emirates Towers is a great place to stay if you aren't into resorts and fellow holidaymakers and desire a hotel that achieves excellence on all levels.

Style 7, Location 8, Atmosphere 8

Kempinski Hotel Mall of The Emirates *(bottom)*
Sheikh Zayed Road, Barsha
Tel: 04 409 5199
www.kempinski-dubai.com
Rates: AED 2,400–39,000

With an average room size of 61 sq m, the Kempinski boasts some of the biggest rooms in Dubai – plenty of space for all those shopping bags. Along with the usual amenities of a five-star hotel, all rooms have the thoughtful addition of a fully equipped pantry and dining area. The Kempinski operates at a high level of service, and offers every business and leisure facility you would expect from a top hotel group, and some you wouldn't – like the Ayurvedic Centre as part of the K Wellness Spa – a refreshing change from the usual 'massage to go' ethos of many hotel spas. The hotel is great for shopaholics, who can get their retail therapy from the mega Mall of the Emirates next door, and families, who want to spend time at Ski Dubai schussing down the

slopes and making snowmen. On the downside, it's not brilliant if you want to spend hours by the pool, which is on the small side for such a big hotel, and the views from the rooms are more urban – unless of course you book a 'ski chalet' for views of snowboarders whizzing by your window.

Style 7, Atmosphere 7, Location 7

La Maison d'Hôtes *(top)*
Villa 18, Street 83B, Jumeirah
Tel.: 04 344 1838
www.lamaisondhotesdubai.com
Rates: AED 850–1,300

This delightful guesthouse in a traditional Jumeirah villa has 20 spacious 25sq. m rooms, all with their own character inspired by the owner's travels throughout Asia and the Middle East. It attracts a euro chic crowd who don't want to do the big resort hotel thing but who like being in Jumeirah. There are 2 swimming pools to choose from, set in pretty gardens overflowing with scented jasmine and bougainvillea. The hotel has a relaxed, pleasant atmosphere and the owners are genuinely interested in making their guests feel at home. An added bonus is the excellent French restaurant (unlicensed), equally popular with Jumeirah locals, small fitness centre and a boutique. The villa is a five-minute stroll to Jumeirah's upscale Mercato Mall and the public beach. Make sure you pop in to the nearby Lime Tree Café for their famous carrot cake.

Style 6, Atmosphere 7, Location 6

Malakiya Villas *(left)*
Madinat Jumeirah
Tel: 04 366 8888
www.malakiyavillas.com
Rates: AED 30,000–38,000

In the heart of Madinat Jumeirah, these opulent duplex 2-3 bedroom villas offer privacy, space, and seriously smart surroundings. Designed in the style of Arabian royal summerhouses, the beautifully appointed villas overlook the waterway that winds throughout the Madinat Jumeirah resort. Chill out on the terrace by your private pool as the butler prepares a martini just the way you like it. The villas have extensive entertaining facilities and feature private water taxi dock, direct access to the Souk Madinat Jumeirah, 24-hour service and all the amenities of one of Dubai's top resorts, including the excellent Talise Spa.

Style 9, Atmosphere 9, Location 9

One&Only *(right)*
Royal Mirage
Jumeirah Road, Al Sufouh
Tel: 04 399 9999
www.oneandonlyresorts.com
Rates: AED 1,250–17,690

This exceptional five-star resort resides along its own private beach among 65 acres of beautifully landscaped gardens, fountains, courtyards and domed pavilions. There are three hotels within the resort to choose from; The Palace is the largest and most atmospheric, Arabian Court the most romantic and The Residence & Spa the most private. Happily, all are superb, so you can't really go wrong. The opulent rooms, with

their traditional Arabian styling, all face the sea and feature private balconies or terraces. During the day the beach beckons with watersports and supervised kids' activities. At night the atmosphere is magical: watch the sun set from the Roof Top lounge, go dancing at Kasbar, and dine like a pasha on Moroccan specialities at Tagine. The spa, one of the best in Dubai, features a luxurious Turkish Hammam as well as Givenchy beauty treatments. A stay at One&Only Royal Mirage is a dream of Arabia straight out of 1,001 Nights.

Style 9, Location 9, Atmosphere 9

....

Orient Guest House *(top)*
Historic Bastakiya Area,
Opposite Al Musalla Post Office
Al Fahidi Street, Bur Dubai
Tel: 04 351 9111
www.orientguesthouse.com
Rates: AED 1,000–1,200

For those seeking a boutique hotel with a genuine Arabic atmosphere, the Orient Guest House in Dubai's historic Bastakiya Heritage area is well worth the hassle finding it. Just look for the sign above a charming traditional two-storey villa – restored to its former glory and offering ten attractive Arabian-style rooms. The roof terrace and two *majlis* courtyards provide tranquil nooks. Staying here gives guests a rare chance to live in the style of the Persian pearl and spice traders who once populated the area, and provides an excellent base for exploring the nearby Dubai Museum, Meena Bazaar, Dubai Creek, Abra Station (water taxi), the galleries and cafes of Bastikiya and all the exotic shops along Al Fahidi

Street. At night, with the moon rising above historic wind towers and cobbled streets, it's as if you've stepped back in time, seeing Dubai as it was at the turn of the century. A delicious Arabic or western breakfast is served each morning and non-alcholic drinks are available (feel free to have cocktails in the privacy of your room). A perk of staying here is the complimentary access to the spa, health club, outdoor swimming pool, bars and restaurants at the nearby Arabian Courtyard Hotel & Spa. Make sure you get detailed directions from the hotel before you arrive.

Style 7, Atmosphere 7, Location 8

....

The Palace *(bottom)*
The Old Town,
Downtown Burj Dubai
Tel: 04 428 7888
www.thepalace-dubai.com
Rates: AED 3,000–35,000

A beautiful new hotel at the heart of prestigious new Downtown Burj Dubai, The Palace radiates Arabian glamour at its most refined. The generous rooms are handsomely decorated in contemporary style, but with classic Middle Eastern touches in the use of regional carpets and woodwork. Butlers are on hand to unpack your bags and grant requests. It's situated next door to all the boutiques and cafés of the Souk Al Bahar and looks out at the stunning Burj Dubai, the world's tallest building. Just across the street is the new Dubai Mall with about 1,200 shops, an aquarium, ice rink, megaplex cinema and more. Although the area is still under construction, it is well worth visiting. There's an inviting pool terrace, Thiptara for gourmet Thai cuisine, and Asado for the best Argentinean steaks this side of Buenos Aires. There's also a very attractive spa with a *hammam*. Service is warm and efficient – the Palace Concierge Joseph David recently won 'Dubai's best Concierge' award.

Style 8, Atmosphere 8, Location 9

 Raffles Dubai *(top)*
Sheikh Rashid Road, Wafi
Tel: 04 324 8888 www.raffles.com
Rates: AED 3,500–45,000

Raffles Dubai is a stunning new addition to Dubai's ever-changing skyline, a postmodern Pyramid in glass and light. Since opening last year it has earned rave reviews for its style – there's a rooftop botanical garden with over 129,000 plants, a library with nearly 1,000 books on Middle Eastern art, history and culture, and the Amrita Spa uses 24 carat gold in its signature facial. The roomy, open plan suites are sophisticated and come with spacious balcony terraces, and 24-hour butler service. Raffles is also home to some of Dubai's top places to wine, dine and party. The Noble House, a contemporary Chinese restaurant with dramatic interiors, won 'Best Chinese', 'Best New Restaurant' and 'Restaurant of the Year'– an amazing hat trick in a city full of good restaurants – and New Asia Bar & Club, a glittering nightclub at the pinnacle of the pyramid. From its terrace, you can look out across Dubai's neon bright cityscape as the city's gilded youth dance to top international DJs. The Amrita Spa is luxurious and has special packages such as the 'Dubai Decadence', six hours of

pure pampering that promises to leave you glossy and glowing. Raffles is right next door to Wafi, probably Dubai's most stylish mall, brimming with boutiques, designer shops, hip cafes and the atmospheric new Souk Khan Murjan, a re-creation of a 14th Century Arabian market.

Style 9, Atmosphere 9, Location 8

 Le Royal Méridien *(bottom)*
Beach Resort & Spa
Jumeirah
Tel: 04 317 6611
www.lemeridien.com
Rates: AED 2,300–12,000

One of Dubai's biggest beach resorts, this five-star playground is perennially popular for its range of activities and waterfront location. Often confused with Le Meridien Mina Seyahi Beach Resort, make sure your taxi knows which one you really want. The hotel is particularly good for families because it caters to all ages and pursuits. Kids can go off for a day of adventures at the Penguins kid's club while mum can escape to the Caracalla Spa and dad can go for a round of golf at nearby Emirates Golf Club. As befits a beach resort, there is a wide range of watersports, including sailing and kayaking. Rooms are pleasant and traditionally furnished, with views of the Arabian Gulf. Don't miss Maya, a stunning, award-winning contemporary restaurant with easily the best Mexican cuisine in the UAE.

Style 6, Atmosphere 7, Location 9

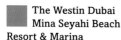 **The Westin Dubai** *(top)*
Mina Seyahi Beach
Resort & Marina
Al Sufouh Road, Jumeirah
Tel: 04 399 4141 www.westin.com
Rates: AED 3,000–14,500

Big, brash and new, with nearly 300 rooms, The Westin's main attraction is its prime position on the beach in sought-after Jumeirah. If you want sand, surf and watersports you'll find it here for less than you would pay at the more exclusive beach resorts. Book a sea-facing room, and the sparkling Arabian Gulf will make up for the uninspired décor. The rooms, featuring Westin's trademarked 'Heavenly Beds', have all the usual amenities, but you will be charged for Internet access. The Westin is home to some excellent places to eat and drink: Oeno wine bar has an eclectic collection of vintages and also offers fine cheeses, tapas and tastings in a dramatic, contemporary setting; the Spice Emporium is a bright and breezy pan-Asian restaurant popular for Friday brunch; while Hunters Room & Grill has a good reputation for its freshly grilled steaks. The water sports centre offers sailing lessons, windsurfing, wake boarding and kayaking, and yacht and speedboat charters are also available. On land, there's floodlit tennis, a gym with a variety of fitness classes, and the Heavenly Spa. Try to avoid booking during school holidays as the resort is very popular with familes on package holidays.

Style 5, Atmosphere 6, Location 8

 **XVA Art Hotel** *(left)*
Bastikiya, Bur Dubai
Tel: 04 353 5383
www.xvagallery.com
Rates: AED 750–900

Dubai's bohemian epicentre, XVA Gallery, has revamped its original guesthouse into an Art Hotel, offering six unique rooms, each decorated by noted regional artists, and all with WiFi, private bathroom and air conditioning. XVA offers visitors a rare chance to stay in one of Dubai's few heritage buildings. The 100 year-old villa in historic Bastikiya has such traditional features as open garden courtyards, wind towers, and *majlis* meeting areas, with views of the Creek. Along with the guesthouse there is the famous XVA Gallery, run by Mona Hauser and considered the source of Dubai's contemporary art boom, as well as a charming café (Gordon Ramsay is a fan of their delicious mint lemonade) and gift shop. Atmospheric and original, XVA will appeal to those seeking a genuine Dubai experience rather than an international hotel chain.

Style 7, Atmosphere 8, Location 8

Serviced Apartments

Arjaan Dubai *(right)*
Media City
Sufouh Road
Tel: 04 436 0000 www.rotana.com
Rates: from AED 2,100

Located in the heart of up-and-coming hotspot Media City and near all the

pleasures of Jumeirah, this is great for those seeking the space, flexibility and privacy of an apartment, with the amenities of a good hotel. Arjaan Dubai Media City apartments (up to three bedrooms) are superbly kitted-out with spacious private balconies overlooking the sea or Dubai's skyline, two LCD TVs, high-speed internet access, master bathroom with shower and bathtub, guest toilet, fully-equipped kitchen, washer and dryer. The private pool apartments are especially impressive. There's also a Bodylines fitness centre with the latest in cardio and strength equipment as well as a temperature controlled swimming pool for adults and an octagonal pool for children set in its own pavilion.

Style 6, Location 6, Atmosphere 6

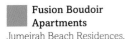

Fusion Boudoir Apartments *(top)*
Jumeirah Beach Residences, Jumeirah
Tel: 050 478 7539
www.fusionhotels.com
Rates: from AED 800

Hip Dubai hoteliers Fusion have recently added five stunning designer apartments to its repertoire, in Dubai's newly fashionable Jumeirah Beach Residences. The area is buzzing with new shops, restaurants and bars – all part what is being called New Dubai. Accommodation is a far cry from the usual dull corporate flat – these apartments are state-of-the-art. Each apartment features two bedrooms (or one bedroom and a fully-equipped office), two bathrooms, kitchen, lounge,

balcony with a breathtaking 180° sea views, and comes fully serviced with breakfast, satellite TV, wireless internet, gymnasium, swimming pool and private beach.

Style 8, Atmosphere 7, Location 8

Harbour Hotel & Residence *(bottom)*
Dubai Marina
Tel: 4 319 4000 www.emirates.com
Rates: AED 1750–4800

Since opening last year, this multi-million dollar combined hotel and serviced apartments concept from Emirates has been very well received. Although Dubai Marina is still under the final stages of construction, the property attracts people from all over the world who want the freedom of a serviced apartment. Guests are especially impressed with the high levels of service and warmth of the staff – in contrast to the impersonal image generally associated with serviced flats. Accommodation is flexible, with anything from a studio to a palatial penthouse available. The apartments are truly spacious and livable in, with sweeping views of Dubai Marina and The Palm. Guests can unwind by the pool, have soothing treatments or work out at the Timeless Spa. The location is excellent for exploring the newly fashionable Dubai Marina, with its chic shops, cafés and restaurants – many have outdoor seating so you can sit back and watch the yachts cruise past.

Style 6, Atmosphere 7, Location 7

eat...

Although it's not entirely true that Dubai is devoid of other evening entertainment, it is fair to say that dining out is something of a national sport. Depending on who you ask, only around 20% of the city's inhabitants are native to the Emirate, and the international cultural melting pot that makes up the rest ensure that the foodie landscape is phenomenally varied, with everything from Al Mahara, the seven star seafood theme park at the Burj Al Arab, to the bonkers backstreet Thai, Smiling BKK.

Most of the restaurants we have recommended here are attached to hotels, and there is a simple reason for that. Bar the odd cunning loophole – the dinner cruise on the Bateaux Dubai, or Century Village's sushi hideout – these are the only places that can legally serve alcohol. The city is well-served with earthier unlicensed options – especially in the higgledy-piggledy streets of Satwa and Bur Dubai – and slipping into a wipe-clean booth at any number of Pakistani, Filipino or Ethiopian joints will often throw up some real gems. These change so often though, and locations are so hard to fathom, that you're better off being a epicurean explorer and locating them by simply pounding the pavements, following your nose – or a hoard of hungry taxi drivers.

Bar the old Arabia stylings of Bastakiah Nights and the desert Disney spectacle of Al Hadeerah at the Bab Al Shams resort, authentic Emirati food is hard to

52

come by. You can't swing a *schwarma* without hitting a decent Lebanese restaurant though and Iranian dishes dot most pan-regional menus, so you won't be Middle Eastern-starved. There really isn't a single country's cuisine that isn't represented here, and if you aren't fussy about your food miles (most ingredients at the higher end of the city's food scale are air freighted) you can easily eat your way around the world in a week.

The city's preoccupation with bigger, better, faster, fatter means that many of the upscale eateries here are characterised by excess. And, for some reason, giant fish tanks. Having spotted that the desert is paved with flash cash, superstar chefs from around the globe – Gordon Ramsay, Nobu Matsuhisa and Pierre Gagnaire to name a few – have all lent their names to venues, with varying levels of success.

If you really want to eat like an ex-pat though, the Friday all-you-can-eat brunches offered at pretty much every hotel are a must-do. Often, they take over all of the hotel's dining locations, offering cuisine from around the world – and, almost without exception, an enormous chocolate fountain. From midday until they decide you've had enough of the free flowing booze (wine and spirits at the cheaper end, branded Champagne if you want to push the boat out), for a flat fee, you can gorge on groaning buffet tables until you can't stand up any more.

the best restaurants

1. Reflets Par Pierre Gagnaire
2. Rhodes Mezzanine
3. The Noble House
4. Zuma
5. The Rivington
6. Nobu *(left)*
7. Empire
8. Rare
9. Bussola
10. Manhattan Grill

1. Reflets Par Pierre Gagnaire
2. Rhodes Mezzanine
3. The Noble House
4. Verre
5. Nobu

1. Reflets Par Pierre Gagnaire
2. Zuma
3. Rhodes Mezzanine
4. The Rivington
5. Empire

1. Al Hadeerah
2. Eau Zone
3. Bastakiah Nights
4. Bateaux Dubai
5. OKKU

Aangan *(left)*
Dhow Palace Hotel, Bur Dubai
Tel: 04 359 9992
www.dhowpalacedubai.com
Open: daily, 12.30–3pm, 7pm–1am
Indian   Dhs200

A *dhow* being a traditional Arabic sailing vessel, you would be forgiven for thinking this five-star hotel boasted a sleepy creekside location. Not so. In fact, it resembles nothing so much as a flouro-lit spaceship that's accidentally landed in the backwaters of Bur Dubai, one of the city's oldest areas. But it is home to a restaurant that constantly crops up in conversation on the best Indians around. Opened in 2006, it was an instant hit with those who appreciate the art of a good curry and with weekend tables often booked up weeks in advance, it's clear that they're still coming. There's nothing exciting about the décor – it's inoffensive carved dark wood and flock wallpaper – but there is live music every night and food-wise, all the old favourites are executed with precision and spiced to perfection.

Food 9, Service 9, Atmosphere 7

....

Al Hadheerah *(right)*
Jumeirah Bab Al Shams
Desert Spa and Resort
Tel: 04 809 6100
www.jumeirahbabalshams.com
Open: daily, 7–11.30pm
Middle Eastern   Dhs500

This open-air dining spectacle, resembling a market scene out of Disney's Aladdin, really puts the case for location, location, location. It's situated an hour's drive from the city centre

(around Dhs100 by taxi – worth it even if only to enjoy sundowners at the rooftop bar) and the postcard desert setting is worth the journey. The low-level cushioned seating provides a perfect vantage point for the theatrical proceedings, namely the Arabian horse show, whirling dervishes, falconry display and camel trot. Oh, and a herd of biddable goats thrown in for good measure. This is the sort of place you won't want to go more than once, as the childlike awe you'll feel on seeing the above for the first time is hard to recapture. As for the food, well it's not the really the point, but the Middle Eastern staples can't be faulted – fish, breads fresh from the oven and charcoal-fired whole lamb – and are served up with panache at the many live cooking stations.

Food 8, Service 7, Atmosphere 9

....

Al Mahara *(bottom)*
Burj Al Arab
Tel: 04 301 7600
www.burj-al-arab.com
Open: daily, 12.30–3pm,
7pm–midnight
Seafood   Dhs800

Located in the bowels of the Burj Al Arab, Al Mahara (meaning pearl in Arabic) is consistently touted as one of the city's most prestigious – and most notoriously expensive – seafood restaurants. Let's just say that the Burj, while undoubtedly luxe, was created when Dubai was definitely more flash than cash. What else could explain the 'submarine' ride that takes you to the restaurant itself? A virtual sea journey complete with lost treasure and

animated fish is not what you'd expect from a seven-star, but it sure is fun. Al Mahara itself, on the other hand, is a lesson in refined elegance, filled with whispering couples bathed in the flattering light of the restaurant's central, conical aquarium. Service is swift, smart and stays on the right side of obsequious. The food generally remains a class act, even if it too errs on the side of kitsch (an ice cream and sorbet dessert served with popping candy feels more Disney than designer). But if you've got a sense of humour and money to burn, an Al Mahara dinner is a Dubai must-do.

Food 8, Service 8, Atmosphere 9

Asado *(top)*
The Palace Hotel, Old Town
Tel: 04 428 7971
www.thepalace-dubai.com
Open: daily, 7pm–midnight. Saturday brunch noon–4pm.
Steak   Dhs400

Although it looks more like a Swiss chalet with the interior design courtesy of Hugh Hefner than a Buenos Aires hotspot, the view of the world's tallest tower (well this week anyway), the Burj Dubai, leaves no doubt as to your location. Take a table on the terrace or sit inside and watch a whole lamb slowly turn on the central *asado* spit the restaurant takes its name from. In a city where service at even the most expensive restaurants often vacillates between incompetent and oppressive, from the knowledgeable sommelier to the waiter that presents you with the raw cuts of cow before they hit the grill, everyone here has been well-trained

and it shows. Steaks, from dainty lady-cuts to slabs as big as saucepan lids, are accompanied by fat-cut chips in a hearty Jenga formation. Saturdays also offer dirty dancing in the form of occasional tango classes and all-the-meat-you-can-eat brunches, where the cuts are carved directly onto your plate.

Food 8, Service 8, Atmosphere 9

Bateaux Dubai *(bottom)*
Dubai Creek, Bur Dubai
Tel: 04 399 4994
www.bateauxdubai.com
Open: boarding starts at 8pm daily
European   Dhs450

It's hard to miss the open-topped bus tours that blight Dubai's rush hours, harder still to understand why anyone would take one ("There's a mall. There's another mall. There's a really big mall with a ski slope"). A much better bet is a ride on the Bateaux Dubai, a glass-walled vessel that delights with a float down the Creek past some of the prettiest parts of the city. There are many other boats that offer the same deal, but few as stylish – the interior is all starched white table linen, low lighting and teak – and none that serve up much other than apologetic *pitta* and flaccid *falafel*. Unusually for a venue outside the confines of a hotel, alcohol is served here but only after you've set sail on the three-hour ride. Once you've found you sea legs, a four-course set menu is served, with breaks in between for photo ops on deck.

Food 7, Service 8, Atmosphere 9

Bastakiah Nights   *(left)*
Bastakiah, Bur Dubai
Tel: 04 353 7772 www.bastakiah.com
Open: daily, 10am–11.30pm
Arabic   Dhs200

Ask any Emirati to recommend the best place in Dubai to eat local food and the fairly unhelpful answer – well, unless they've taken a particular shine to you – will be 'my house'. Press further and they may well suggest this unlicensed restaurant, one of only a handful to specialise in the cuisine. Set in the city's oldest district, it's a bit of a trial to find – although small, the area's low-rise, sand coloured buildings are pretty much indistinguishable from each other as they seem to have decided signage would spoil the old Arabia aesthetic – but take a seat in the open-air courtyard or one of the several small rooms that adjoin it and you'll be transported into a sanitised 1001 Nights fantasy. Heavy, carved wood doors, glowing torches, berry-coloured wall-hangings and more scatter cushions than a mid-sized Ikea all add to the low-lit charm. The mountains of food the set menu send to the table are Himalayan, so unless you're ravenous, the á la carte – where Iranian, Emirati and Lebanese dishes all jostle for space – is a less belt-loosening option.

Food 7, Service 7, Atmosphere 10

Bussola   *(top)*
The Westin Dubai Mina Seyahi, Al Sufouh Road
Tel: 04 399 4141
www.starwoodhotels.com
Open: daily, noon–2.45pm, 7–10.45pm
Italian   Dhs300

Confusingly, this stand-out Italian was previously attached to the next door hotel, accessible via a golf buggy across the beach. But the newly-opened Westin pinched this prime location on opening in 2008. Luckily, that's all that's changed about this seafront stalwart. Set on two floors, the more laid-back, open-air top level serves probably the best thin-crust pizza in the city while the kitchen below sends out more refined fare. Here, the menu is long – though helpfully, starts with a one-page chef's selection of house specials. The pastas – which go heavy on the bacon (none of your strange smoked beef and turkey substitutes here) – are always perfectly *al dente*, but if you're not in the mood to carb-load, there's lobster and steaks aplenty. The wooden terrace is a prime spot on a balmy night, but the floor-to-ceiling glass windows of the indoor space mean it's packed year-round.

Food 7, Service 8, Atmosphere 9

Eau Zone   *(right)*
The One&Only Royal Mirage
Tel: 04 399 9999
www.oneandonlyresorts.com
Open: daily, noon–3.30pm, 7–11.30pm
European   Dhs500

You might think, given its 'ya-boo, we've got more beach than you' Palm location, that the Atlantis would trump its sister resort with waterfront dining options. But, while it might be true that at the Royal Mirage you can't feast with the fishes, at Eau Zone you'll see enough first dates making goggle-eyes eyes at each other that you can pretend. Accessed via a wooden footbridge, the tables on the wooden platforms (outside of the scorching summer months) are textbook romantic – proper first date fodder, complete with flickering tealights and traditional *majilis* canopies. The food is rich and French-influenced, with an emphasis on seafood, and the large puddings decadently butter-laden; this is one place you won't mind if your 'oh, just a camomile tea for me' date launches *crème brûlée* blitzkreig with her teaspoon.

Food 8, Service 8, Atmosphere 9

Empire *(top)*
The Monarch Hotel,
Sheikh Zayed Road
Tel: 04 501 8888
www.themonarchdubai.com
Open: 7–10.30pm Sun–Thurs
European   Dhs900

From the hotel that boasts one of the city's most expensive hotel suites, you'd expect a fine dining experience of epic proportions – and the evening-only Empire doesn't disappoint. Understated it is not, but the sparkling crystal chandeliers, chocolate and bronze velvet banquettes and gold-rimmed plates bring a particularly sophisticated blend of bling. The head chef greets and talks guests through the constantly-changing hand-written menus, but won't throw too much of a hissy fit if you decide to go off-piste. The cooking offers the sort of bells-and-whistles gastronomy that usually justifies these sort of prices in Dubai – supplemented by *amuse bouches* with showy flourishes of steaming dry ice and test tubes of soups and syrups that are theatrical enough to compete with the opulent setting – but the kitchen is also assured enough to let the top-notch ingredients speak for themselves, with French-influenced Wagyu, *foie gras* and truffles all taking centre stage.

Food 9, Service 9, Atmosphere 9

Fire & Ice *(bottom)*
Raffles Dubai
Tel: 04 314 9888   www.raffles.com
Open: daily, 7pm–midnight
European   Dhs900

This place is so-named because of its extreme-temperature approach to food preparation: a dramatic curtain of flame surrounds the open kitchen, and much of the meat on offer is singed in pans at sub-zero temperatures rather than cooked in the conventional manner. Sure, there are a lot of other novelty twists – a preponderance of bright, frothy foams and even a course of *foie gras* topped in ten-cent popping candy – but a backbone of superlative cuts of marbled meats and the freshest fish means that these come off as pleasing, artful flourishes rather than pretentious window dressing. The sommelier has somehow assembled a list to complement the kitchen's every wacky eventuality and, if you select the set menu with a different wine for each of the (many) courses, you'll be toasting your wise choice of restaurant well into the early hours.

Food 9, Service, 7, Atmosphere, 9

Frankie's *(top)*

Oasis Beach Tower
Tel: 04 399 4311
www.frankiesitalianbarandgrill.com
Open: 12.30–3.30pm Thurs–Sat, 6pm–
11.45pm daily
Italian   Dhs200

It's advisable to book ahead at this Dubai outpost of the nascent chain set up by Michelin-starred chef Marco Pierre White and Italian jockey and sometime Dubai-dweller Frankie Dettori. At weekends it can be difficult to even get standing space at the bar, let alone an impromptu dinner at one of its pleasantly shadowy tables. There's a whiff of the gentlemen's club about the décor, which is all walnut wood and cappuccino walls, but on your way to the *pissoir* check out the slightly troubling framed snap of giant Marco with his hand rammed into little Frankie's pants. If that doesn't put you off your food, you'll find a menu packed with the classics (think pizza, pasta, risotto) alongside more innovative takes on the Italian culinary lexicon and a well-thought out and reasonably-priced wine selection.

Food 8, Service 8, Atmosphere 8

Lemongrass *(middle)*

Oud Metha
Tel: 04 334 2325
Open: daily, noon–11.15pm
Thai   Dhs100

With its copy shops and office chair warehouses, the area surrounding Lamcy Plaza, Dubai's frumpiest shopping experience, where the likes of (whisper it quietly) BHS are relegated, doesn't inspire confidence as a place for culinary discovery. But unlicensed Lemongrass is a shining, indy green beacon in these chainstore badlands. There are two or three tables on the balcony outside, but unless you're a chain smoker or exhaust enthusiast, avoid as they afford only a view of the car park opposite. The waitresses are friendly and helpful, but there's not much on the menu that needs explaining. They will quiz you as to the spice level required level of the curries, noodle dishes and standard starter fare. Smoothies are standout, offering fruity holistic goodness – just ignore the fact that the first one on the menu promises to soothe those nasty stomach upsets.

Food 8, Service 9, Atmosphere 7

Manhattan Grill *(bottom)*

Grand Hyatt
Tel: 04 317 1234
Open: daily, 12.30–3pm, 7–11.30pm
Steak   Dhs400

It's a testament to the charm of the gargantuan Grand Hyatt's dinky steak spot that it manages to give a whiff of New York while being overlooked by the cathedral-like hotel lobby's main talking points – the huge hulls of three traditional *dhows* and an almost Kew-sized selection of tropical vegetation below. As the great steak debate ranges on in the city – for some reason, it seems be the Dubai-dweller's favourite foodstuff – this stalwart continues to draw in a crowd of faithful diners. Although the décor is pleasant enough – chrome, glass and dark wood, with an open kitchen at the back of the room – what this restaurant really adds to Dubai's steakscape is its impeccable mastery with meltingly soft cuts of imported meat, a must-eat for committed carnivores.

Food 9, Service 9, Atmosphere 8

 **Momotaro** *(left)*
Souk Al Bahar
Tel: 04 425 7976
Open: daily, noon–midnight
Japanese   Dhs200

In true 'knock it down and build a better one' style, one of Dubai's favourite 'historical' souks was actually opened in 2008 and can boast traditional Arabic delights including a Starbucks and a Cinnabon. Bypass these though and you'll find it also offers some of the city's finest dining options, which have the added bonus of not being attached to a hotel. Momotaro, in the bowels of the building (the journey involves several escalators, a bridge, a tin man and some flying monkeys. Not really.) has made a name for itself as one of the finest. The black-and-red room, which could fall into the oriental tat trap, actually comes off as a sleek, streamlined space. The wait staff is attentive and the food imaginative – sushi and sashimi staples of the highest quality sit alongside more outré examples from Wagyu California rolls to *foie gras*. The only trouble is, over-indulge in the wide range of sake on offer and you might need to tap your red shoes three times to find your way home.

Food 8, Service 9, Atmosphere 7

 **The Noble House** *(right)*
Raffles Dubai
Tel: 04 314 9888   www.raffles.com
Open: daily, 7–11.30pm
Chinese   Dhs900

Chances are you'll already have seen into The Noble house – albeit from a great distance. Any cross-town taxi trip is likely to afford a view of the Raffles pyramid, inside which sits Dubai's finest Chinese dining experience. The lighting in this red-and-black restaurant is on the gloomy side of moody – but don't worry, you'll be led by experts every step of the way. The gymnastic welcoming tea ritual is performed by a man that trained for five years in order to achieve the requisite contortions and this sets the tone for an evening of exquisite culinary excess. The well-spaced tables hug the glass walls so every diner can gaze down upon the twinkling lights below but your eyes are just as likely to remain on your plate, as scene after scene of masterpiece culinary theatre unfolds there. Forget everything you thought you knew about Chinese cuisine, from the shark's fin soup to the *foie gras* dim sum, The Noble House re-invents the wheel with honours.

Food 10, Service 9, Atmosphere 9

Nobu *(bottom)*
Atlantis The Palm
Tel: 04 426 0760
www.atlantisthepalm.com
Open: daily, 7pm–midnight
Japanese   Dhs700

The Dubai outpost of the restaurant that made black cod an A-list fish is

destination dining in the most literal sense – first there's the journey to the centre of the Palm, then to the restaurant itself (you have to walk past the resort's gob-smacking tank, stuffed with thousands of fish. Oh, and a whale shark that one day will be as big as a double-decker). It's an odd way to whet your appetite for an evening of piscine indulgence, but worth it for the sort of sushi that's made chef Nobu Matsuhisa almost as famous as the chain's co-owner, Robert De Niro. The dark, cave-like dining space is essentially a big square room, which affords a view both of the sushi chefs at the long counter and also the slightly odd mix of clientele – which range from baseball-capped Americans staying in the 2,000-room mega hotel to the occasional banker and be-frocked It girl. The food – all of the star dishes have made it onto the lengthy menu – and service is worth the trip and two-month wait for a table.

Food 10, Service 9, Atmosphere 7

 OKKU *(top)*
The Monarch Hotel, One Sheikh Zayed Road
Tel: 04 501 8777 www.okkudubai.com
Open: daily, 7pm–3am
Dhs400   Japanese

In a city that boasts more private zoos than it does pet dogs, it's maybe unsurprising that live, nature doc-style entertainment has become de rigeur in Dubai's nightspots. So clever old OKKU for carving a niche as the place to seen and be seen – by, erm, loads of jellyfish. Yep, the star attraction in this restaurant-cum-cocktail bar is a UV-lit 'jellyquarium'. With such a show-stopping water feature located behind the talented mixologists' heads, you'd be forgiven for thinking that the food wasn't really the point here. Until you take a seat at one of the low-level tables or prop up the sushi bar and your perfectly-prepared Japanese fusion food arrives, that is – the rock shrimp is a revelation and the chocolate fondant dessert is worth the visit alone. For VIP privacy, the plush upstairs tables can be completely blocked off from prying eyes – yes, even from the jellyfish.

Food 8, Service 7, Atmosphere 8

Persia Persia *(bottom)*
Wafi City
Tel: 04 324 4100
Open: daily, 12.30–3pm,
7.30pm–midnight
Iranian   Dhs250

Tucked away in the eating annexe of Egyptian-styled Wafi mall, which comes complete with a ten-foot Ramases and Styrofoam pyramids, this Iranian restaurant is a surprisingly under-designed oasis. Sunken seating areas and copious cushions offer reclining options for pre- or post-prandial cocktails (which you may need – the portions are huge and the food stream almost endless) but a table on the terrace, which overlooks the swimming pool of an expensive ex-pat residence below, is a pleasant option in summer months, especially if you want to partake of a *shisha* pipe. More expensive than its spit-and-sawdust Satwa rivals, the Persian food – a cuisine so often overshadowed by its Lebanese cousin – here is excellent; the breads are freshly-baked, grilled meats are gristle-free and the *meze*-style starters generous.

Food 7, Service 7, Atmosphere 8

....

Rare *(left)*
Dubai Desert Palm,
Al Awir Road
Tel: 04 323 8888
www.desertpalm.com
Open: daily, 7–10.30pm
Steak   Dhs500

The drive out to this hotel, perched on the edge of a polo pitch, will give you the impression you're heading out into the desert. And, strictly speaking, you are. But, the minute you pull into the driveway you'll be enveloped by an incongruous oasis of lush greenery that annually plays host to polo's global cognoscenti for the Cartier Cup. The carnivorous clientele is largely made up of moneyed ex-pats with sprawling villas the other side of the pitch or post-game players, here to enjoy serious cuts of steak. The house speciality is Wagyu, cooked on the wood-fired grill, which comes with an army of side dishes that make good use of the big, well-spaced tables. Make an evening booking here and it's only the twinkling Burj Dubai beyond that will suggest the sandy city you're in.

Food 9, Service 9, Atmosphere 8

....

Reflets par *(right)*
Pierre Gagniere
The InterContinental Festival City
Tel: 04 701 1128
www.intercontinental.com

Open: 7pm–midnight.
Closed Saturdays.
European   Dhs800

The approach to this well-babysat outpost of the Michelin-magnet chef's international empire (all too often, world-class chefs of Pierre's ilk lend their name and make for the bank without much thought for aftercare) makes you feel like James Bond being led into Q's subterranean lair: the restaurant has its own lift, and the purple carpets are accented with sniper target insignia. Once inside, you might feel, however, that 007 has lowered himself from frighteningly elegant Russian ice queen to Paris Hilton. It's all Venetian mirrors, hot pink booths and tremendous fun. Waiting staff have an encyclopaedic knowledge of the ever-changing menu and even the well-travelled foodie will find surprises. If you're lucky, the affable restaurant manager will talk you through the Daliesque *amuse bouches*, which are constructed from whatever's been flown in from Europe in the last few hours. Abandon all hope of sparing food miles: Reflets is a plane-to-plate kind of place and a fine example of the 'molecular gastronomy' that Gagnaire is credited with creating.

Food 10, Service 10, Atmosphere 8

....

Rhodes Mezzanine *(bottom)*
The Grosvenor House
Tel: 04 399 8888
www.grosvenorhouse-dubai.com
Open: daily, 7.30–midnight
European   Dhs500

This bright white room, with its padded leather walls, resembles nothing

so much as a Starck-designed lunatic asylum – in a good way, of course. The third-floor location doesn't afford a view of much other than the building site opposite, so the white organza drapes which encircle the restaurant provide a much more pleasing aspect, with the brightly-coloured button-back chairs and flouro yellow window into the kitchen adding splashes of colour to what could otherwise be a bland space. The food is spiky-haired Michelin-star holder Gary Rhodes' take on British, so expect rib-sticking dishes like pork belly and jam roly poly, along with unbidden *amuse bouches* that constantly appear on the table. It you want to sample everything he does best, order from the tasting menu's roll call of mini palate-pleasers which can be tried individually.

Food 9, Service 9, Atmosphere 8

Rivington Grill *(top)*
Souk Al Bahar,
Downtown Bur Dubai
Tel: 04 423 0903
www.rivingtongrill.ae
Open: daily, noon–11pm
Dhs300   British

The Middle-Eastern outpost of London's Rivington Grill is an oasis of laid-back chic – white butcher's tiles line the walls, broken up with cool neon signage, with an open kitchen serving piping-hot dishes over a marble countertop at which you are welcome to sit when it's rammed (which it almost always is). The food is essentially great gastropub grub – fish and chips, steak, dressed crab and a wicked Eton Mess and sticky toffee pudding are signa-

tures – and the wine list is excellent and incredibly good value. But it's the service that will knock you sideways – smiling, efficient and knowledgable. Brunch here is unfailingly brilliant – it's the only place in Dubai that does a decent Welsh rarebit. During cooler months, request a table on the terrace to enjoy it. You'd be advised not to do the same in the evenings though, as once the Dubai Fountain it overlooks cranks up, you'll need a cagoule and a golf brolly.

Food 8, Service 10, Atmosphere 9

Ronda Locatelli *(bottom)*
Atlantis The Palm
Tel: 04 426 0750
www.atlantisthepalm.com
Open: daily, 1pm (noon Fri/Sat)–3pm
and 6–11pm (midnight Fri/Sat)
Italian   Dhs400

Dubai's bonkers, partially submerged Atlantis, nicknamed 'The Eighth Chunder of the World' by one inventive tabloid in its opening week, is full of eateries, all of which are currently stuffed to the rafters thanks to the hotel's sheer notoriety. Although some of them (the steak canteen Seafire, for example) will have to up their culinary and hospitality game if they want to maintain these levels of occupancy long-term, Ronda Locatelli has got it right from the start, with a solid spread of peasant favourites culled from Giorgio Locatelli's London 'Locanda' flagship. As well as the pasta-and-rice classics, there's a selection of thin and crispy pizzas prepared at the giant four-station furnace which dominates the dome-like space. It may be less ritzy than its European forbears, but in a hotel that looks like it was conceived for Posh and Becks, it's solid, rustic charm is something to treasure.

Food 8, Service 7, Atmosphere 8

Il Rustico *(left)*
Rydges Plaza, Al Diyafah Street
Tel: 04 398 2222
Open: daily, noon–3pm,
6pm–midnight
Italian   Dhs150

Long-time Dubai-dwellers go all misty-eyed about this little Italian. Set in the sort of hotel you're unlikely to give a second glance unless you've been told, it achieves the unusual feat of making you forget that the rough stone walls are cladding and the foliage fashioned from plastic and feel like you've stumbled upon the sort of trattoria that mamma used to frequent. Solid, reasonably-priced traditional dishes made from good quality ingredients (lots of pork in case you're feeling pig-starved) are the mainstay of the menu. If you're on a date, avoid the garlic bread that arrives, steaming, to the table almost instantly – they use a whole head per loaf. Do make like the Lady and the Tramp though and share a main course bowl of pasta or a pizza – they're seriously super-sized.

Food 7, Service 6, Atmosphere 8

Segreto *(right)*
Souk Madinat Jumeirah
Tel: 04 366 8888
www.madinatjumeirah.com
Open: daily, 7–11.30pm
Italian   Dhs400

Strictly speaking, dating is illegal in Dubai. Unless you are in possession of particularly tech-savvy cells, you'll even find that trying to search for your soulmate online will send your laptop into lockdown. So the couples in this secluded corner of Madinat Jumeriah are all, of course, just good friends. Or related. Regardless, if you want to moon over your, ahem, brother, then this is a mighty fine place to do it; snuggled in the elegant main dining room – split into nooks by lattice-work screens – you will almost certainly secure a second non-date. The food is trad Italian, gussied up with glam ingredients – think *osso bucco* lasagna – and the European wine list is long. In summer, if you bag a sought-after balcony table overlooking the waterway, you'll want to add mosquito to spray to the pheromone melee but in the winter helpful staff hand out pashminas to ward off the breeze.

Food 8, Service 9, Atmosphere 9

Shabestan *(bottom)*
Radisson SAS Hotel,
Dubai Deira Creek
Tel: 04 222 7171
www.deiracreek.dubai.radissonsas.com
Open: daily, 12.30–3pm,
7.30–11.30pm
Iranian   Dhs150

eat...

Rumoured (well, more like advertised by the maître'd) to be among Sheikh Mohammad's favourites, Shabestan offers sophisticated Persian dining in the shadowy seclusion of Deira's Creekside SAS Radisson. The faded, by Dubai's standards, grandeur of this hotel contributes to the impression that Shabestan (meaning underground space) is about class rather than just brass. Most nights there's entertainment in the form of unobtrusive *oud* strumming and gong wobbling; food flavours are similarly delicate and the service is immaculate, with just the right amount of time left between the issue of variations on the house staple: steaming portions of rice and meat. The mutton, stewed in a clay oven, is a favourite, as are the cute baby chickens. It's all surprisingly light on the pocket, as well as the stomach, and the *vermicelli* and rosewater dessert is enough to make you nostalgic for Iran,

even if you've never been.

Food 8, Service 8, Atmosphere 8

Smiling BKK *(above)*
behind Al Wasl Road, Jumeirah
Tel: 04 349 6677
Open: daily, 11am–midnight
Thai   Dhs100

Tucked away behind the Emarat petrol station on Al Wasl Road, next door to a copy shop that literally prints money, this can be a toughie to find; but persevere and you'll be smiling too by the end of the night. Quirky doesn't do justice to this nutty joint serving 'Number 1 Awesome Food in Town' (even if they do say so themselves). Don't come starving, as you'll need to block out a good 15 minutes for giggling over the adorably smutty dish names – will you be having a '1 Night

in Bang Cock' (spicy sour soup) with an 'Amazing Thai Lady!!' (prawn and lemongrass soup) or would you prefer 'Pussy Cat Got Wet' (stir fried chicken with fried garlic), sirmaam? The décor is similarly eccentric – from a nude oil painting adapted with Shariah-compliant swimwear to the outside toilets which are pure Phuket.

Food 8, Service 7, Atmosphere 10

Sushi Sushi   *(above)*
Century Village, Garhoud
Tel: 04 282 9908
Open: daily, noon–midnight
Sushi   Dhs150

The nostalgic stylings of the Irish Village pub which dominates Garhoud's Century Village, with its faux tobacconist and strings of all-season party lights, looks so much like a plaster-

board film set one can completely forget to look behind it. Those who make the journey around this gated leisure development's circumference will be rewarded with a secret Costa coffee franchise (hardly The Beach, is it?), a so-so steakhouse and this magnificently pokey sushi hideout. A cute conveyor belt sequesters the chef at the back, but the best seats in the dollhouse are the cosy window-side sofas. It really is a novelty to be offered a drink with your meal when not dining in a hotel, so take advantage, order a few rounds of Asahi or Sapporo and get stuck in to the delightfully substantial fish food. Monday night's all you can eat sushi deal is particularly gratifying.

Food 7, Service 7, Atmosphere 9

Teatro *(left)*
Towers Rotana Hotel,
Sheikh Zayed Road
Tel: 04 343 8000 www.rotana.com
Open: daily, 6–11.30pm
International   Dhs250

In a place where restaurants open at an alarming rate, it's rare to find one that keeps locals coming back for more. Teatro – housed in a hotel that sits among Sheikh Zayed Road's proliferation of fast food joints – is one such gem, necessitating a booking days in advance at the weekend. In comparison to its neon-lit neighbours, it's a theatrically-themed, eclectic space with heavy drapes, deep banquettes and a glass-walled wine cellar. The main reason for the place's enduring popularity with chattering groups of young expats though is the fact it neatly avoids the 'what shall we have tonight?' dilemma by cooking a cross-continental offering. This jack-of-all trades approach often proves to be a risky strategy, but here it's all cooked with an assured hand, so the sushi, Chinese, Indian and Italian are all equally impressive.

Food 8, Service 7, Atmosphere 8

Thai Kitchen *(right)*
Park Hyatt Dubai, Deira
Tel: 04 602 1234
www.dubai.park.hyatt.com
Open: daily, 7pm–midnight. Brunch noon–4pm Fridays.
Thai   Dhs200

In a city where show kitchens in up-scale hotel eateries seem to come as standard, Thai Kitchen reminds the tired throng how it should be done,

with piles of shining exotic fruit on ice and pristine chefs performing at dinky, distinct show kitchens dotted around an airy space, which doesn't have two clichés to rub together. In more temperate months, head outside by the calming Creek to experience one of Dubai's finer *al fresco* dining options. The motto here is little and often, so order up a storm of delicately flavoured mini-dishes, which stretch far beyond the realms of spring rolls and *satay*. The place also has one of the best value Friday brunch deals. For an all-inclusive fee, you can order limitless fare, freshly cooked – a salve for those tired of the boozy buffets that characterise Dubai's weekend kicks.

Food, 8, Service, 8, Atmosphere, 9

Verre *(bottom)*
Hilton Dubai Creek, Deira
Tel: 04 227 1111
www.gordonramsay.com/dubai
Open: 7pm–midnight.
Closed Saturdays.
French   Dhs600

Gordon Ramsey led the first wave of Michelin-starred chefs into Dubai and at Verre that shows. Not just in the consistency of what comes out of the kitchen but in the setting and surrounds. Its location at the Hilton Dubai Creek is a good indication of its age – as Dubai has rapidly grown southwards, this spot is most firmly now the wrong side of the water – while the room itself, all sleek chrome and glass, lends a decidedly 90s feel. All these are mere quibbles, however, in the face of the fare on offer. Ramsay, despite spreading his talents more thinly than the finest filo, keeps a firm reign on his operations around the globe, and his Dubai outpost is no exception. The current chef, Mark Pickup, moved here from Claridge's and has brought with him all the brilliance of fine dining in the English capital. You may not come here for the atmosphere but, with a menu boasting dishes such as the signature halibut with lobster and herb risotto, and what has to be Dubai's perfect *tarte tatin*, you'll definitely return for the food.

Food 9, Service 10, Atmosphere 7

■ **Zuma** *(right)*
■ DIFC
Tel: 04 425 5660
www.zumarestaurant.com
Open: daily, noon–3pm,
7pm–midnight
Japanese   Dhs600

The business district location of this, the fourth in the international chain of upscale modern Japanese eateries, means that during the day it attracts men with fat wallets and expensive suits, and in the evening, the thin ladies who love them. It's only fitting that this 300-cover, two-floor glass cube of a joint retains its status as the place to see and be seen (epitomised by the 'private' goldfish-bowl style dining room which hovers in the high-ceilinged space), but even the impressive eye candy pales in comparison to what's on your plate. There are stools arranged around the sushi and sashimi station so you can watch the skilled chefs slice and dice the air-freighted fish. The giant traditional *robata* grill

serves up succulent *yakitori*, Wagyu and even – usually for Dubai – your common-or-garden veg dishes.

Food 9, Service 9, Atmosphere 10

drink...

There are many misconceptions about drinking in this Muslim country, so let's just lay one to rest straight off the bat. You can. And people do, often in vast quantities. In fact, Dubai can boast many and varied establishments from Rock Bottom, where you can order your kebab in the same breath as your beer, to top-flight Champagne bars like Eclipse, where you literally have the world (or an Emirate, at least) at your feet.

The biggest obsession when it comes to watering holes here is a view – so leave the beer goggles at home as you'll be paying through the nose to look down it from a great height. In a place where the city is an attraction in and of itself, you'd be missing out if you didn't visit at least one – the newly-opened Neos is the big boy on the block (it's a whopping 63 floors up), but Vu's and Uptown Bar have been packing them in for years. The clientele here is seriously moneyed, wearing their labels on their sleeves (and their feet, and their wrists) and throwing their cash around like they own and oil well. Which it's more than likely they do.

Thursday and Friday are the weekend nights in Dubai and the most popular places are packed to the rafters. As everyone travels in taxis anyway, bar-hopping – even to the other side of town – is the done thing and the punters are never knowingly underdressed. Even at beachside bastion Barasti, girls sink their stilettos into the sand.

The one thing that they all have in common though is that they are all attached to hotels – even if slightly tenuously. No back-street speakeasies in this town.

Mosaic Chill (right)

The Agency *(left)*
Souk Madinat Jumeirah
Tel: 04 366 8888
Open: daily, 6pm (5pm Fri)–1am
(2am Thurs)

The branch of this suited-and-booted wine bar in Dubai's financial centre has been open for ten years, but unless you are particularly fond of bankers with their ties loose and tongues looser, the Madinat outpost is preferable. Instead of the DIFC's view out over a couple of escalators and its distinct drink-in-a-mall vibe, this bar has a moody, torch-lit interior and an outdoor terrace that overlooks the winding waterways below from a lofty height. It's quite hard to find – the Madinat's winding alleys can be difficult to negotiate, but clearly many manage as it's spectacularly popular and always packed with happy locals and tourists sensible enough to bypass the Starbucks. Hang around for a table and you'll be rewarded with an epic wine selection, gourmet international tapas and even a gooey cheese fondue.

Après *(right)*
Mall of the Emirates,
Sheikh Zayed Road
Tel: 04 341 2575
Open: daily, 10am–1am

Obviously every international ski resort needs a little après spot to warm the cockles after some downhill action, right? Although few would expect a desert to be home to a real snow slope (actually there are soon to be two – and 2009's version will have polar bears and penguins), the Mall of the Emir-

ates' prime attraction – where grown-ups can pelt down the hill on skis and kiddies can steal each others' sleds in the snow park below – is kind of convincing, in an odd way. And so, too, is this Alpine-themed bar, complete with stone-clad walls. Set at the foot of the slopes, it's a great vantage point for the inept snowboard stylings of punters in their blue-and-red Michelin man suits. It makes a pretty mean cocktail too, and the food – pizza, burgers and fondue – is top-notch. The best views are from the bars stools, but once you've had an eyeful, sink into one of the white leather booths.

Bahri Bar *(bottom)*
Mina A'Salam Hotel,
Madinat Jumeirah
Tel: 04 366 8888
Open: daily, 4pm–1.30am

Many of the watering holes surrounding the Madinat afford a decent view of the Burj Al Arab, but this is one of the few where you are pretty much guaranteed to find a seat, indoors or out, from which you can see its garish light show without craning. The first floor bar's name means 'of the sea' and it does what it says on the tin, with a wraparound terrace that's perched above Al Qasr's own stretch of water. Apart from Friday, when rowdy post-brunch punters (Al Qasr's is one of the most popular in Dubai) flock to prop themselves up against the bar, this is an elegant yellow-and-cream, art deco-style spot, ideal for a sundowner cocktail and a sharing plate of *mezze*.

Barasti *(top)*
Le Méridien Mina Seyahi
Tel: 04 399 3333
Open: daily, noon–1am

Nicknamed 'Bar Nasty' by some of Dubai's more discerning drinkers, this is nonetheless one of the only true beach bars in town and if you pick your moment, it's actually rather nice. Especially pleasant on Saturday, when the boob tube brigade is at home racking their brains for the name of last night's shag. Pitch up mid-afternoon and chances are you'll be able to pounce on one of the big white sofas at beach level and stick your toes in the sand, or secure a table on the terrace above from which you can stare at the Palm. On weekend nights, you're well advised to get there early as the queues can snake round the corner. It's shoulder-to-shoulder air stewardesses dancing to the surprisingly good covers band and downing Jaegerbombs after midnight – good old fashioned cheesy fun if you're in the mood.

Buddha Bar *(middle)*
Grosvenor House,
Dubai Marina
Tel: 04 399 8888
Open: daily, 8pm–2am

Don't even think of trying to slip past the baying mob at this Dubai outpost of the Paris super-club without a reservation. It's not that they won't let you in – they will, after looking you up and down a few times and making you stand like a plum behind the velvet rope – but to fit in amongst the Porsche-owners and posh frocks you'll need to dress to the nines, and nobody wants to sweat on their Friday best. There's a more staid restaurant section up the back serving sushi, Chinese and decent Thai food. But, bar-wise, if you actually want to have a conversation, sit in one of the sofa-filled ante-rooms that flank the entrance corridor; the volume in the warehouse-sized central room, with its super-high ceilings, is consistently turned up to 11. The décor is oriental-by-numbers, with the bar's namesake deity presiding beatifically over the beautiful people and the Marina they overlook.

Belgian Beer Café *(bottom)*
Crowne Plaza Festival City
Tel: 04 701 1111
Open: daily, 4.30pm (noon Fri/Sat) –2am

No prizes for guessing what this place does best. Attached to Festival City's two-in-one mega hotel, it's the place to head for a Hoegarden, a slug of Stella or a dizzying (literally, if you try to taste them all) variety of yeasty nectar – in fact, if you like your beverages brown and bubbly, there really isn't a better destination in Dubai. For a theme pub, it's remarkably untacky and expensively done up, with wall-mounted bric-a-brac, tin signs and battered leather suitcases, lit by brass chandeliers. The Friday brunch – unlimited beer and breakfast from 11am, with piles of freshly-baked bread, pots of steaming mussels and artery-clogging delights appearing after midday – is heartburn-inducingly hearty. Oh, and the toilets are worth a mention for the fact that they look like they've been airlifted from a rural Victorian prep school.

drink...

Bidi Bondi *(top)*

Clubhouse Al Manhal,
Shoreline Apartments, Palm Jumeirah
Tel: 04 427 0515
Open: daily, 10am–midnight

There's nothing especially inspired about the décor at this primary-coloured Palm hangout, but that doesn't much matter as it's a prime place for beautiful people spotting. The bar stools, booths and wall-mounted surfboards inside are pleasant enough, but it's a seat on the bar's terrace that's the most hotly-contested on a warm afternoon. On the ground floor of an apartment complex, you have the benefit of the resident's pool to peer at (and sneak into, it you're feeling brave), surprisingly lush (for a desert) gardens and a long stretch of man-made beach. Breakfast is served from 10am if you're an early riser or want to be sure to get an outdoor table, and if you can bear to say the names out loud, a lunch or dinner of Chook Salad or Roo Wrap (made with your actual kangaroo) are filling enough to soak up the wide selection of draught beers.

The Cellar *(left)*
Century Village
Tel: 04 282 4122
Open: daily, noon–1am

Come Thursday night, this is the after-work hangout of Dubai's self-styled media whores, but don't hold that against it. Next to the airplane-shaped Emirates building (oh, to be a fly on the wall at that planning meeting – 'It should be big! Yes! And airplane-y!'), it resembles nothing so much a mid-nineties yuppie bar plopped into a sub-urban Baptist church, complete with stained-glass windows. Set in Century Village, opposite the raucous Irish Village, a pub-slash-concert-venue, take a seat on the spacious terrace and you might catch a set by Bob Geldof if you're really unlucky. When Saint Bob's not screeching, it's a fine place to enjoy an al fresco draught beer and a sensible selection of mid-priced wine. Bar snacks are booze-soakers, not dainty bites, from the same kitchen as provides the restaurant's oft-excellent grub.

Cin-Cin *(right)*
The Fairmont Hotel,
Sheikh Zayed Road
Tel: 04 332 5555
Open: daily, 6pm–2am

In comparison to more recently-opened, design-heavy hotels, the Sheikh Zayed Road's Fairmont is a bit of a relic. But once you've made it past the pretty unimpressive lobby and up to Cin-Cin, it loses the dowdy carpet and becomes a much sleeker space. It's managed to retain its see-and-be-seen atmosphere in this fickle city, and consequently still attracts the unbuttoned shirt brigade looking to spend their bonuses on the attendant tottering totty. A seat at the bar provides a good vantage point for this testosterone circus, but the mix of sink-into seating in the long, curved space is difficult to resist. The wine list is long and pocket-emptying, with most wines available by the glass. Food is *foie gras* and caviar heavy, as you might expect.

Crossroads Bar *(top)*
Raffles Hotel, Oud Metha
Tel: 04 324 8888
Open: daily, 5pm–2am

The pretty botanical gardens that sit on the rooftop of Raffles are the backdrop for one of the bar scene's best-kept secrets. More laid back than its shiny counterpart China Moon, it's ideal if you want to hear yourself smoke – the outdoor terrace is all but silent and an ideal spot for a contemplative *shisha*. If you don't want to sample a trademark Singapore Sling – invented at the hotel's sister location – you can try the Dubai version or one of the spirits on the impressive list. The Balinese-themed indoor space is less atmospheric.

Eclipse *(left)*
InterContinental Festival City
Tel: 04 701 1111
Open: daily, 6pm–1am

If you come to this 26th floor bar at sunset, you'll enjoy one of the most fabulous views of the twinkling city any Dubai establishment has to offer. Sure, at weekends it can be full of guys looking girls in short frocks and high heels up and down instead of surveying the scene outside, but during the week, a seat at one of the tables by the windows that encircle the bar is a pretty great spot. The red-and-black décor, all swirling carpets and glittery granite, is decidedly late 80s, but manages somehow to be sleazily retro, not screamingly naff. The wine and Champagne menu is expansive – and expensive – and the cocktails several levels above most local bars, where a *mojito* can often resemble warm Sprite garnished with limp mint.

Ginseng *(right)*
Wafi City Mall, Bur Dubai
Tel: 04 324 4777
www.ginsengdubai.com
Open: daily, 7pm–1am (2am Tues–Fri)

At first glance, this Asian-themed bar might appear a bit of an odd proposition, but persevere (the only other dining option in the immediate vicinity is Planet Hollywood, so I daresay you will regardless). It's one of the older drinking spots in the area, and as such its red-and-black pan-ethno décor has stared to look a little scruffy round the edges. It's still an impressive space though, with high ceilings, a back wall given over entirely to backlit bottles and tall velvet banquettes encircling the room. The young, fun crowd that habitually head there to drink their way through the vast, well-priced cocktail list and line their stomachs with really rather good noodle, rice and sushi dishes, most of which come in vast sharing plates, still clearly appreciate it. The music, which can be slightly ill-chosen at times (pumping house music at half past eight) is often drowned out by choruses of Happy Birthday as the assembled crown get merrier.

Harry Ghatto's *(left)*

Jumeirah Emirates Towers,
Sheikh Zayed Road
Tel: 04 330 0000
Open: daily, 8pm–3am

Dubai's drinkers aren't a 'hide their light under a bushel' bunch, so the weekend scenes at this karaoke bar are always of a dad-at-a-wedding standard. In fact, you can usually hear the enthusiastic (but often less than tuneful) efforts emanating down the escalators in the eerily empty mall way before you hit the front door. Big it ain't, but that doesn't stop the punters climbing on the banquettes (and then being told to get down again) to see the incongruous video accompaniments to the televised lyrics. It takes a while for your song to come up, and be prepared for a microphone scuffle with an inebriated secretary if you happen to have beaten her to *I Will Survive*. But it's always packed with lively groups of drinkers who have spilled over from the surrounding offices to sup on sake and imported beers.

iKandy Ultra Lounge *(top)*

Shangri-la Hotel,
Sheikh Zayed Road
Tel: 04 405 2703
Open: daily, 6pm–2am

The bottom of Sheikh Zayed Road is not a place you'd expect to have its own mini Ibiza, so the recently-opened iKandy is still a bit of an insider find. Its moniker might be the nomenclature equivalent of an 'If you think I'm beautiful…" T-shirt, but the boasting is right on the money most nights, with a flashy, pretty (or should that be pretty flashy – this joint is not cheap) clientele ordering tapas, smoking *shisha* and tapping their feet to the resident DJs. You'll find even those not thwacked with the pretty stick look palatable, as the ultra-violet glow means you'll see everything through oddly rose-tinted spectacles. Set around the fourth floor pool deck, the extra eye candy also comes in the form of a great view of the gigantic Burj Dubai

Left Bank *(right)*

Souk Al Bahar, Old Town
Tel: 04 368 4501
Open: daily, noon–1am

This glam watering hole could be tricky to find, bar the fact that you can usually see its 'one-out-one-in' queues snaking round into the mall come 8pm. Its sister branch in Madinat Jumeirah has long been the go-to place for a quiet glass of vino in a pretty setting, but this Old Town location has trumped it. The interior is moody and opulent, with metallic flock wallpaper and an abundance of dark nooks and plush booths, although you may need to hover a while before you can secure one. The cocktails are delicious and imaginative and the food, which comes in dainty mini-portions, is above-average bar fare. Unlike some Dubai hotspots, it's very easy to see why this has quickly become a firm favourite with the locals – be warned though, its popularity means it can afford to be picky on the door – so bin the flip flops.

Mosaic Chill *(top)*

The Kempinski Mall of the Emirates, Sheikh Zayed Road
Tel: 04 409 5999
Open: daily, 7pm–2am

In a city where the weather ranges from rather hot to very hot, there are surprisingly few locations that offer beer-in-hand poolside lounging. This new bar attached to Dubai's favourite mega-mall is a shining example of how it should be done. From the outside, it doesn't look up to much – and certainly the only view you'll get from the third floor is of the 10-lane highway below, but then you won't be peeking over the side much. Cross the perilous-when-pissed over-water walkway and you'll find a louche lounging spot where you can smoke *shisha* while listening to a DJ spinning the sort of tracks that make the largely Lebanese crowd whoop with joy. Although you aren't encouraged to jump in, the bottom-lit swimming pool is a very pretty backdrop for the beanbag-strewn bar.

Neos *(left)*

The Address, Old Town
Tel: 04 436 8888
www.theaddress.com
Open: daily, 5pm–2am

If Dubai's newest mega-hotel wasn't dwarfed by the gargantuan Burj Dubai next door, it would easily be one of the tallest buildings in the city – it's certainly the best-lit, its mega-watt blue-and-white neon making it visible from space. Probably. Calabar, its poolside, sister watering hole is a much more low-level affair, while Neos is high-octane and very, very high up. From the 63rd floor you have a spectacular view over the city's central (and often clogged) artery, the Sheikh Zayed Road, and an insight into quite how quickly the thousands of workers and forest of cranes have made Dubai the Middle East's New York. Reached by its own elevator from the 61st floor, Neos screams money – it's all chrome, giant chandeliers, button-backed banquettes and slightly snooty staff dressed in designer gowns – and you'll need to be prepared to spend your own. Not even looking is free here – on Thursdays and Fridays they levy a Dhs100 cover charge on – but it is a stonking location.

Oeno *(right)*

The Westin Mina Seyahi, Al Sufouh Road, Dubai Marina
Tel: 04 399 4141
Open: daily, 4pm–1am

The Westin's Oeno takes its wine seriously and, unusually, doesn't overcharge for it. The novel-length list has been culled from all over the world, with everything from New World sparklers to heavy French reds, and the knowledgeable sommeliers are thrilled to be asked their opinion. The lofty room has a mezzanine level, which features some particularly space-age sofas, but a bar stool on the ground floor is preferable, as most nights there is a good jazz trio working the grand piano. At weekends, the young crowd can be slightly noisier than this classy cream-and-white room might expect – in fact, it's not unknown for an over-watered oenophile to try and scale the five-metre high wine wall. Cheese-freaks are well catered for with a wonderful walk-in *fromagerie*, housing an encyclopaedic, ever-changing collection to accompany the grape-based drinks.

drink...

Rock Bottom *(left)*
Regent Palace Hotel, Bur Dubai
Tel: 04 396 3888
Open: daily, noon–3am

Rock Bottom is a bar with its own kebab stall for erm, Bottom feeders. Need I go on? Actually, I better had as, for all this pool-bar-cum-boozer-cum-*schwarma* stand gets knocked, it is the stealth favourite of many an after-hours party lover. It's actually not a bad place to stop off for a more sober steak and chips during the day even though it quite closely resembles a suburban Harvester, complete with chequered tablecloths and sticky carpets, but it's after dark that it really gets down and dirty. Some might say it's a bit of a pick up joint, and it's difficult to argue, but that's more because by the time everyone – and here that means Hell's Angels, media whores, sailors, daddy's little girls and anyone else who stumbles in – has tucked into a few of their signature Bullfrogs (basically a top shelf with added Red Bull – yum) they're in a great mood and up dancing to the rebel rousing nightly band.

Rooftop Terrace *(bottom)*
One&Only Royal Mirage
Tel: 04 399 9999
Open: daily, 5pm–1am

A trip to this cushion-strewn rooftop hangout is a leisurely experience. It's actually set over two levels, but the best sipping spot, predictably, given the name, is accessible by rose petal-strewn stairs and affords a sterling sea vista. In fact it's one of the only places in town that you can get a real sense of quite what an odd island the Palm really is – looking out over the Gulf, you can see the multi-lane highway that leads out to the footballers' favourite frond-end villas and identikit apartment blocks that resemble nothing so much as an elongated council estate. Set around a central, igloo-shaped dome with eerily-lit lilac portholes, there are low-level tables dotted about in the open air and big square booths under vast pergolas. Service can be slow, but you'll almost certainly stay here well into the wee hours, so just sit back and relax.

Sho Cho, *(right)*
Dubai Marine Resort, Jumeirah
Tel: 04 346 1111
Open: daily, 7pm-3am

Probably the most beautiful collection of Lebanese outside of Beirut, you'll be hard pressed to single out any unattractive drinkers or even those with an ounce of spare body fat at this late-night beachside hangout. It's consistently completely rammed, even on a Sunday when the DJ deigns to bust out the eighties tunes. You can sit inside, but nobody does, preferring to stand shoulder-to-shoulder on the ocean-side deck. Split into three sections woe betide anyone who becomes confused – turn left and you've got the mega-spenders, their tables groaning with bottles of vodka, right and it's diners chucking back sushi and shouting conversation and in the middle, Joe Plumber and his gang enviously wishing they could head in either direction. The door tends to be guarded by the usual surly bouncer frowning disapprovingly on every single male, no matter how chiseled, but will happily wave past couples or mane-tossing girls with a grin.

The Terrace *(top)*
Park Hyatt
Tel: 04 602 1234 Dubai.parkhyatt.com
Open: daily, noon–2am

You might get an inkling as you drive up the lengthy approach, but take one step onto the terrace at the Park Hyatt and you'll immediately see why it trumps all other hotels this side of town in terms of location. Parked right on the Creek, with a view of the Marina where a fair few disgruntled millionaires own moorings (which the majority bought before they erected the 'floating' bridge, effectively trapping their water-bourne palaces for most of the week) it's an oasis of calm. This largely outdoor bar has an air of Miami, with roomy cream sofas under appropriately sail-shaped awnings – and if you don't manage to grab one of those, there's always a table on the expansive decking. Wine and Champagne are the order of the day, and the food a few notches up from standard bar snacks – oysters, caviar and fat prawns sit atop ice chips at the glass-walled indoor bar.

Trader Vic's *(left)*
Mai Tai Lounge
Oasis Beach Towers,
Marina Walk, Dubai Marina
Tel: 04 399 8993
Open: daily, 6pm–2am

There's no point even pretending that this Polynesian-themed joint is classy, but boy is it fun. Even during the week, the noise from the assembled happy ex-pats can be deafening, and that's before you add the live Cuban band into the cacophony. Housed in a strange mini mall – you have to go up an escalator, then walk past a Wagamama and a fur coat shop (yes, apparently even people who live in 50 degree heat covet vicuna) – it's not the most salubrious of locations, but once inside the Tiki tat will win you over. The ceilings are high, the bars clad with bamboo, and the wicker chairs have a 70s holiday resort vibe – plonk yourself down on one, order a goldfish bowl-sized cocktail (some of which come with decidedly illegal-in-Dubai half-naked plastic dolls swimming in them) and some of the excellent Asian-influenced bar snacks.

Uptown Bar *(right)*
Jumeirah Beach Hotel,
Jumeirah Tel: 04 406 8181
Open: daily, 7pm–2am

The glass elevator ride to this rooftop bar is a bit Charlie and the Chocolate Factory and the payoff every bit as sweet. This 24th floor stunner rides the crest of the wave-shaped Jumeirah Beach Hotel and despite its astounding view of the Sheikh Zayed Road to one side and the sea on the other, it's rarely packed. The psychedelic carpets and questionable scarlet colour scheme you're assaulted with on entry might make you doubt your choice until you step outside and realise that those that are in on the secret are right to be smug. It really is a gem – and one of the few places in the city this high-up that you can sit outside and enjoy the slight-less-smoggy air. The pretty epic cocktail list is well executed across the board, and bowls of bar snacks arrive as soon as you sit down. And, of course, it's particularly stunning at sunset.

Vu's Bar *(above)*
Jumeirah Emirates Towers
Hotel, Sheikh Zayed Road
Tel: 04 330 0000
Open: daily, noon–2.30am

Although it's recently been knocked off the top spot in terms of views (if you'll excuse the pun), the slightly seedy 51st floor of what used to be Dubai's tallest building is still an interesting, if over-priced, place to quaff a Champagne cocktail. The clientele is an unusual mix of men in local dress and women of sometimes questionable moral repute, plus a few tourists and escapees from the office block opposite (where Sheikh Mohammed, the Ruler of Dubai, used to have a few floors to himself). It's a shiny-shoes-and-shirts destination – the dour doormen will have no issues with turning you away if they don't deem you properly dressed. The tables by the triangular windows (a theme throughout the building, apparently influenced by Islamic astronomy) are the best as you'll have to crane to see the Dubai's lightshow below otherwise.

Telephone Numbers...

snack...

If you spend much of your time wondering where Emiratis go after leaving the mall and while you are chowing down on your five-course booze-laden evening foodfest, the answer is simple: the city's many unlicensed cafés. Sitting street-side with a *shisha* and enjoying that Arabic staple - coal-tar coffee with sweet, squidgy dates - is one of the favourite weekend past-times of a good portion of Dubai's local populous.

The locations of the most popular snack spots are a good reflection of how Dubai divides its time. Those that aren't in hotels – and we haven't included many of them here as eschewing booze means a much more varied choice of destination is possible – tend to be centred around the waterfront and shopping malls. The latter shouldn't make your heart sink – stopping to refuel whilst laden with bags is actually a pretty good bet, as Momo's Almaz (shown in the photo opposite) and the Gold and Diamond Park's own More café prove. The waterfront locations – The Boardwalk, Bait Al Wakeel and Bistro Madelaine - are a relaxing way to spend an afternoon away from sandy building sites too. For cake, coffee and a salad, the yummy mummy throngs congregate at the more chi-chi venues like the Lime Tree Café and More, where the outdoor tables are often circled by pampered mini pooches. For something really laid back why not try the poolside Epicure (right) at the Desert Palm.

For snacking on the go, forget the standard fast food joints – and there are more than you could shake a Big Mac at, with all the big international chains from Taco Bell to New York Fries well represented – although some, like Beirut's Zatar W Zeit are worth a visit, and Johnny Rockets serves hands-down the best burgers in town. If you are in a hurry, the city's many Lebanese bakeries are great for a super-cheap cheese *mankish* or *falafel* wrap. Spice fiends will find curry cravings amply satisfied at the spit-and-sawdust Ravi's or Deira's Karachi Darbar. And anywhere you see a pavement, you'll almost certainly spot a hole-in-the-wall juice café, serving ice-cold vats of freshly-squeezed juice for pocket change.

snack...

Al Mallah   *(left)*
Al Dhiyafha Road
Tel: 04 398 4723
Open: daily, 6am (noon Fri/Sat)–3am
(4am Fri/Sat)

With precious few pavements to its
name, Dubai is largely devoid of street
life, which makes Al Dhiyafha a bit of
a diamond in the rough. Lit largely by
neon signs announcing fast food joints,
at night the street imparts an eerie glow
to the boy racers who cruise between
the roundabouts at either end, showing
off their fast cars to anyone who cares.
Al Mallah, by dint of being open later
than all the rest of the *mezze* joints in
town and colonising much of the road
with it extensive outdoor seating, is an
ideal vantage point for this Hummer
grand prix. It also happens to serve a
mighty fine – if snack-sized – *schwarma*,
which comes daintily wrapped in
white paper for even the most inel-
egant (read: drunk) of eaters. Try the
dense *falafel* dripping with *tahini* and
rainbow-coloured fruit juices too, all
helpfully (if slightly unappetisingly) described by photographic menus.

Almaz by Momo   *(bottom)*
Harvey Nichols,
Mall of the Emirates
Tel: 04 409 8877
www.harveynichols.com
Open: daily, 10am–midnight
(1.30am Fri)

Mourad Mazouz, the man that made
Moroccan hip in London, has lent his
skills to this stylish, sprawling eatery
that houses a juice bar, *shisha* café and
central dining salon. The low lighting
and North African pop music make it
feel a lot like its British cousin Momo,
but as this is Dubai, the champagne is
necessarily non-alcoholic. In fact, it's
only the fact that Almaz is unlicensed
(erm, and in a mall) that prevents us
from recommending it as an evening
hang-out, as the food and service are
top-notch. As it stands though, it's a
great place to avoid the Mall of Emirates' (yes, the one with the ski slope)
weekend hoards of screaming brats in
salopettes, with the delicately spiced
couscous, *tagines* and *pastilla* for the
shopping-weary, and mint tea and
tooth-hurting pastries offering a dizzying sugar rush.

Bait al Wakeel   *(right)*
Bur Dubai
Tel: 04 353 0530
Open: daily, noon–midnight

Ignore anyone that turns their nose
up at this place and tells you it's just
for tourists – they're probably just trying to head you off at the flume queue
at Atlantis. In the bustling old part
of Dubai, it's the only fairy-lit eatery
hanging over the water, and so pretty
easy to spot, but keep an eye out for
the nearly-concealed entrance. The
mezze – *falafel*, *kibbeh* (balls of chopped
meat and spices) and piping hot
sambousek (stuffed pastries) – are all as
good as you'll find at most Lebanese
cafes and are cheap and filling. The
shisha and fresh juices are fine too,
but they're not the reason you'll want
to linger. From every single one of the
outdoor tables, you get a great view of
the Creek and the *dhows* that sail up
and down it. It's a charming spot and

snack...

105

best reached by *abra* – a budget two minute ride across the Creek – and a far preferable water-based ride to a shark-infested death slide.

....

Basta Art Café *(left)*
Bastakiya
Tel: 04 353 5071
Open: daily, 8am–10pm

This charmingly eclectic outdoor café is the sort of place you could spend a whole afternoon, sipping fresh juices and camomile tea. The courtyard is shaded by a large, central tree (unusual in a city dotted with spindly palms) with cloth canopies hanging from it, hiding guests from the midday sun. The mis-matched furniture is comfortable enough to lounge on for hours, with a battered paperback. The building itself is actually one of the city's oldest, built 100 years ago by an Iranian merchant and situated next to Dubai's least impressive monument – an old bit of tumbledown wall, reverently described by a dusty plaque. The service can sometimes be confused, but it's hard to get annoyed with the smiling staff who offer up huge glass bowls of home-made salad and tasty sandwiches. When temperatures climb into the forties, there is a cosy, cushioned *majilis* to lounge in.

....

Bistro Madeleine *(right)*
InterContinental Festival City
Tel: 04 701 1128
www.dubaifestivalcity.com
Open: daily, 8.30am–11pm

Squint and you might think this chic French brasserie was on the banks of the Seine and not Festival City's fast-developing marina. Its rag-rolled, tobacco-coloured walls are lined with art nouveau posters, the bent-wood bistro chairs are dark-stained wood and the red velvet banquettes make you feel you should be flouting the smoking ban with an unfiltered Gauloise whilst humming *Je ne regrette rien*. All the classics are name-checked on the menu that reads like a Gallic greatest hits – from *foie gras* pâté and French onion soup to the obligatory *croque monsieur*. The well-executed food is made with top of the range imported ingredients, born out by the fact that should you happen to give your compliments to the chef he will probably hold forth on the fine-grade flour they fly in from France just for the fluffy baguettes.

....

The Boardwalk *(bottom)*
Dubai Creek Golf Club, Garhoud
Tel: 04 295 6000 www.dubaigolf.com
Open: daily, 8am–1am

Sure, it can be difficult to attract the frantic waiters' attention for a refill and the quality of the food rarely matches the Creekside location, but boy, what a location it is. After journeying Dubai's Mall network in a hermetically sealed car the size of a Winnebago, the possibility of stretching one's legs, watching the *abras* meander across the still water and the gentle cackle of seagulls is a delightful novelty indeed. OK, so it's not exactly back to nature, but in this town it's as close as you're going to get, so suck it up. The burgers and sandwiches are reliable time-fillers.

Don't be tempted by the fancier fare, though: returns diminish as the chef's aspirations climb. No matter. When it comes to hanging around, The Boardwalk simply can't be beat.

Central Perk *(left)*
Uptown Mirdiff
Tel: 04 394 8081
Open: daily, 10am–1am

Like the Cheers bar in London's Piccadilly Circus, this franchised coffee shop is an anachronistic flashback to a sitcom of yesteryear. You might be forgiven for not expecting much of an establishment affiliated with the actor who played the Germanic, largely mute Rachel-devotee Gunther in nineties blandathon Friends, but in actuality, you could do a lot worse than the steaming lattes, giant blueberry muffins, eggs Royale and not-particularly-English full English breakfasts on offer here. The residential Uptown Mirdiff location is a handy auto stop-off between the chaos of Bur Dubai and the ritzier hotel-based offerings down the other end of the Sheikh Zayed Road. A place this mainstream is unlikely ever to be cool, even in a deeply ironic way, but it's a nice place to indulge in spot of nineties nostalgia before it becomes the norm. Also found in Jumeirah.

Courtyard *(right)*
Al Manzil Hotel, Old Town
Tel: 04 428 5888
www.southernsunme.com
Open: daily, 6pm (noon Fri/Sat)–2am

Oddly, this is one of the few places in Dubai where it's still possible to sit outside comfortably in the height of summer. Whether it's the high-rise, faux-olde-Arabic hotel that it sits slap-bang in the middle of shielding you from the blazing sun or the overspill from the air-con inside, this accidental micro-climate makes it the perfect place to sit and enjoy *meze* and *shisha* on a balmy night. Service can be a little slow and it's such a hot ticket (excuse the pun) that most nights you might have to wait a while waiting for a table, but once ensconced, you'll want to linger.

Curry On *(bottom)*
La Plage Complex,
Jumeirah Beach Road
Tel: 800 287799
Open: daily, 11.30am–11.30pm

As crammed as Dubai is with impressive Indian eateries – from show-off fusion food to tin-plate, bargain basement chow – it's unlikely you'll leave many with a spring in your step. For a lighter bite, ignore the crap pun and Curry On up Beach Road to this spice emporium that essentially peddles poppadoms for girls. Set at the back of a little courtyard, it's a sweet space with a menu that reads like a 'Greatest Hits' of sauce-based world cuisine. Green curries, *kormas* and *rendags* all jostle for attention on the menu but luckily you don't have to chose be-

tween them – they're helpfully bundled together in tasty trios, so that you get three little complementary portions all bursting with flavour. All in all, a much less gout-inducing proposition.

Dean and Deluca *(left)*
Souk al Bahar, Old Town
Tel: 04 420 0336
Open: daily, 11am–10pm

This Emirati outpost of New York's hip deli and café looks as if it simply sashayed out of the pages of "Sex and the City". There are 'It' bags casually slung on stainless stools, dishy young men talking shop on their mobiles and, of course, extravagantly hued cupcakes under immaculate glass domes. It's self-service in a point and smile kind of way, and you might have to wait a few minutes for a table at the weekend (D&D is one of the only units in Souk Al Bahar to have escaped the deserted 'nuclear winter' vibe) but persevere and you'll be rewarded with some of the freshest produce in town. Share a Manhattan paving stone sized eggplant pizza slice between two, and supplement with a couple of bespoke salads and you'll have experienced one of the oil state's most enjoyable refuellings.

Emporio Armani Caffé *(right)*
Mall of the Emirates
Tel: 04 341 0591
Open: daily, 10am (2pm Fri)–11.30pm (midnight Fri)

We all know Mr Armani cuts a mean suit, but who suspected he could also slice a mean sandwich and conjure up a wicked *ganache*? On the first floor of this mega-mall, this first-floor black-and-orange eatery is a calming pitstop, offering better than average Italian fare, from San Pellegrino, salads and *carpaccio* if you're planning to fit into a size zero, to more standard pizza, pasta and *gelati* bar if you're not on the supermodel diet.

Epicure *(bottom)*
Dubai Desert Palm,
Al Awir Road
Tel: 04 323 8888 www.desertpalm.ae
Open: daily, 7am–11pm

There's something of the Ibiza boutique hotel about the infinity pool at the Desert Palm, and Epicure's floor-to-ceiling windows afford a fine view of the beautiful people lazing in it on chic floating beanbags. Don't let their lithe limbs put you off tucking into the sublime café-style offerings here, though. The bright interior, which could be garish were it not executed with such a great eye for colour, is breezy and perfectly suited to all-day lounging. There's a long counter with barstools at which you can perch and read the lifestyle-envy inducing magazines strewn over it. The menu covers all bases, from Welsh rarebit to egg-white omelette and heartier offerings like duck leg curry, Wagyu steak sandwiches and thin-crust pizzas, a favourite with regulars, the Dubai Harley Davidson Group. Yes, really.

snack…

Fish Basket *(left)*
Bur Dubai
Tel: 04 336 7177
Open: daily, 10am–1am

The most important thing to remember about this functional fish bar tucked away behind the more glamorous confections of the Garhoud Bridge is that its servers don't know the meaning of the word small. In common with the rest of Dubai's Lebanese eateries, you need only set foot in the place to be presented with a massive complementary veg platter that wouldn't look out of place atop Carmen Miranda. Reign in the more extravagant designs of the men behind the choose-your-own fish counter, and you'll be able to fill a sizeable hole with sparklingly fresh seafood without having to resort to money laundering. Grilled shrimp is particularly good value. Although this unlicensed restaurant can appear a bit glum by day, a nocturnal visit during holiday season is rewarding: the massive Sheikh Zayed portrait rug next to a flashing synthetic Christmas tree is one of the finest Middle East-meets-West quirky snaps to be had in a city full of such photo opportunities.

Johnny Rockets *(bottom)*
Marina Walk
Tel: 04 368 2339
Open: daily, noon–midnight

Who could fail to love a restaurant where, at periodic intervals, the entire staff drop everything (not literally, thankfully) and break, cod-spontaneously, into a synchronised routine to Staying Alive? A little disconcerting if you've just walked in, but take a seat on one of the red vinyl booths at this retro American diner regardless – just resist putting money into the mini-jukebox on the table as sadly it won't speed up the Saturday Night Fever Megamix. Instead, peruse the concise list of the best burgers in town. These perfect patties are grilled right before your eyes at the long counter by bow-tied staff – when they're not doing their John Travola impersonations, obviously – and topped with juicy slices of tomato, melting cheese and bacon smoked so well you won't believe it's bovine. N.b. It is. Branches are also to be found at Mall of the Emirates and Juma al Majid Centre, Jumeirah Beach Road.

Lime Tree Café *(right)*
Jumeirah Beach Road
Tel: 04 349 8498
www.thelimetreecafe.com
Open: daily, 7.30am-6pm

The Jumeirah Jane is a remarkable breed. Better groomed than their Brit counterpart, the Sloane, and with a deeper tan than their Park Avenue Princess sisters, they single-handedly keep the Beach Road's beauty salons in business and the Lime Tree in eye candy. Small dogs, big sunglasses and huge blow-dries are *de rigeur* on weekdays, but come the weekend, this two-floor villa-cum-café is where Dubai's under-30s come to dissect the night before. It's best to hunt in pairs at peak times here – split up and send one to stalk that sought-after, shaded table on the upstairs terrace while the other stands in the always epic (but

usually fast-moving) queue. Choose from a huge English breakfast (served until 1pm at the weekend) that's as good as a porkless fry-up can be or try the lighter lunch fare – salads, quiche, sandwiches and frittata – that's laid out in front of you behind a glass counter. Go for the carrot cake – it's attained near-mythical status.

More Café *(left)*
Al Murooj Rotana
Tel: 04 343 3779 www.morecafe.biz
Open: daily, 8am–10.30pm

More by name, more by nature – anyone who leaves this place without a lunchbox of leftovers clearly hasn't eaten for a week. The four branches (and counting) of this permanently packed institution prove you can be a culinary jack of all trades. The many-paged menu, which comes helpfully bolted to a square of hardboard, plucks dishes from right across the globe, each tackled with equal assurance, from *nasi goreng* and lasagne to Thai green curry and *Wiener schnitzel*. At weekends, the sociable central tables which feature in all branches come ready-strewn with newspapers, all the better to peruse over a pot of cafetière coffee that will please aficionados (eight different blends are offered). For the truly ravenous, the non-boozy brunch, with its constantly replenished silver platters will undoubtedly have you coming back for, erm, More. Further outposts to be found at Al Garhoud; Gold and Diamond Park; Sheikh Zayed Road.

The Noodle House *(right)*
Jumeirah Emirates Towers
Tel: 04 319 8758
www.thenoodlehouse.com
Open: daily, 8am–1am

While the rest of the world has been falling for the charms of Alan Yau's Wagamama (to which the UAE has only recently cottoned on) Dubai has been going crazy for The Noodle House, a delightful pan-Asian concept with similar brisk, efficient service, reasonable prices and high quality ingredients – but without, thank goodness, the uneasy canteen benches. Tick your selection of wet noodles and soups, wok fried noodles, specialties and side dishes from your order pad, hand it to your server and wait all of five minutes before the intense flavour hits the top of your nostrils. The system works so well, it's no wonder Sheikh Mohammed, ruler of Dubai, is rumoured to be a fan. Don't neglect the delicious and inventive list of mocktails: together with the *bakmi goring* with chicken and prawns, these constitute ex-pat UAE's hangover cure of choice. Branches also at: Deira City Centre Mall; Souk Madinat Jumeirah; BurJuman Mall, Bur Dubai.

Organic Foods and Café *(bottom)*
Satwa
Tel: 04 398 9410
www.organicfoodsandcafe.com
Open: daily, 9am–8pm

Dubai lags behind much of the world in its interest in organic – in supermarkets, you'll be stared at blankly if you ask for free range eggs and enquiries about the pre-*pitta* life of your chicken *schwarma* will elicit a snort of derision. Thus, this Satwa stalwart has earned itself a place in the little black books of the Emirate's health-conscious. Attached to an organic supermarket, selling everything from shampoo to shellfish and freshly-baked bread, this café makes impressive use of its neighbour's prime ingredients to produce home-cooked staples. It's a fairly sparse space – all white drapes, blonde wood and terracotta floors and a few 'socks-and-sandals' murals – but certainly pleasant enough for a lingering breakfast or lunch stop. The best value is the Friday brunch, where you can fill your boots with breakfast, salads and quiche from 11am for an all-inclusive price.

Ravi Restaurant *(top)*
Satwa
Tel: 04 331 5353
Open: daily, 5am–3am

There aren't many Dubai cheap eats that a taxi driver will find without a lot of pointing and several distressed calls to colleagues. Ravi Restaurant, however, will earn you a smile, a nod and a stress-free journey, as it's fairly likely he'll be a regular. There are no airs and graces at this local institution, which serves perfect Pakistani food to the masses. So popular is it – poll locals and you'll probably find more have set foot inside this Satwa landmark than have visited the Burj Al Arab – you'll likely have to hover round looking shifty and being offered 'genuine fake deeweedee' until a space at the outdoor, wipe-clean tables is vacated by a sated customer. Epic over-ordering is

part of the fun but you'll still struggle to spend more than peanuts on the mounds of mutton *biryani*, succulent kebabs and feather-light breads that arrive as and when they emerge, piping hot, from the kitchen.

Sezzam *(bottom)*
Kempinski Hotel,
Mall of the Emirates
Tel: 04 409 5999
www.kempinski-dubai.com
Open: daily, 11am–11pm

This expansive, but not expensive, collection of live cooking stations is set at the bottom of Mall of the Emirates' Ski Dubai mountain, and its operators have wisely injected a dose of theatre into the food preparation in order to avert your gaze from the enormous dividing window and the trippy on-slope antics beyond. At weekends, there are clowns, face painting and a bouncy castle for the kids, while adults get to create hitherto unattempted taste combinations from the global fare on offer for an all-inclusive price. The concept can get a little confusing (pizza and smoothies, for some unknown reason, are excluded from the weekend Sezzam Express brunch option) but it's all part of the sensory overload which characterises the place. Visit after, rather than before, an afternoon's shopping: too much mud pie and marshmallow from the amazing dessert counter and you'll be temporarily immobilised.

The One Café *(top)*
Jumeirah Beach Road
Tel: 04 345 6687
www.theoneplanet.com
Open: daily, 9am–9pm

If dining in a furniture store summons up visions of Ikea meatballs, this glam deli-style café will surprise and delight. The enormous Beach Road branch of the UAE's chicest interiors chain has won awards for its fusion cuisine, but a recent refit, replaced the black vinyl chairs and dark glass chandeliers with white leather sofas and wooden tables, and the menu has joined the revamp too. The breakfast – which they will serve at any time, should you roll out of bed post midday – ranges from freshly-baked banana bread to granola via more rib-sticking option of eggs Benedict. The rest of the café's creations are displayed behind the glass counter, where you'll find salads, sandwiches, homemade cheesecakes and peanut cookies. Delicious but dangerous if you're planning a trip to the beach across the road.

Shakespeare & Co *(right)*
Village Mall,
Jumeirah Beach Road
Tel: 04 344 6228
Open: daily, 7am–12.30am

This local chain is a love-it-or-hate-it sort of place. The décor looks like someone's let their maiden aunt lose in a suburban Oxfam – the beaded lampshades, chintzy sofas and heavily flocked wallpaper are the fusty side of eccentric – but if you find it all too oppressive, there is an enormous ter-racotta-tiled terrace to escape to. Even on Friday, when the rest of this bou-tique mall is a ghost-town, Shakespare & Co is packed with locals who clearly don't think the food is much ado about nothing. It's a great quick coffee stop, with glass counters piled high with gleaming patisserie and sherbet-co-loured macaroons to greet you as you walk in. If you're after something more filling, the exemplary Arabic breakfast and more standard sandwiches, pastas and crêpes are not bard at all. OK, I'll stop now. Branches also to be found at Sheikh Zayed Road; Al Wasl Road; The Meadows and Gulf Towers; Oud Metha Road.

Wafi Gourmet *(left)*
Wafi City Mall, Oud Metha
Tel: 04 324 4433 www.wafi.com
Open: daily, 10am–midnight

Granted, the view from the frou frou terrace here looks like something from one of those 'crap postcard' collec-tions (it's an enormous car park plus a dystopian cluster of residential tower blocks) but the mock-Egyptian stylings of the restaurant's bonkers interior will keep you entertained nevertheless. A cross between Harrods food hall and a nineteenth-century Oriental market scene, Wafi Gourmet has mountains of olives, chocolates, jellies and sweet-breads for the take-home customer plus *shisha*, meat kebabs and mountains of glistening *fattoush* (salad) for those wanting to down anchor mid shopping spree. Order sparingly if you're plan-ning to make another lap around this maze-like mall: you'll be assailed with industrial quantities of flatbread on

entry, and main portions are generous. The fresh fruit shakes make for an elegant pit stop treat. Boiled lamb's brain? Not so much.

XVA Gallery Café *(top)*
Bastakia

Tel: 04 353 5383 www.xvagallery.com
Open: 9am–7pm. Closed Fridays.

In the past few years, the art market in the Middle East has begun to boom. Most of the big-name galleries are located in the Al Quoz area, which can be difficult to find and even harder to navigate, filled as it is with unremarkable, unmarked warehouses. In sharp contrast, Bastakiya, which is now a wipe-clean rendition of what it once was, (namely the hub of a city that, a century ago, was just a small trading port), you'll find the XVA gallery. One of the gems in this almost eerily empty area, it's a leading light in the burgeoning art scene and also boasts one of the prettiest courtyard cafes in Dubai. The vegetarian fare is cheap as chips but much, much healthier and with an onsite mini-branch of glam fashion boutique S*uce, it's a whole lazy Saturday in one manageable dose.

Zaatar W Zeit *(bottom)*
Sheikh Zayed Road
Tel: 04 80 092 2827
www.zaatarwzeit.net
Open: daily, 24 hours

The traditional Lebanese breakfast pizzas, served at the Dubai cousin of this Beirut-based chain, are a bit of an acquired taste – the original rosemary-topped bread should not be attempted with a hangover as, with a mouth already starved of moisture, it feels a bit like eating tasty sand. Ironic really, as this place is open 24/7 and is a bit of stalwart for a post-pub, booze-sodden bite – they even deliver, so if you find yourself at home and lacking in lard it's a perennial option (though of course you risk waking up to find yourself face-down in one on the sofa). It also stands up to consumption when in full possession of your faculties – there are many variations on the theme served here (the theme being bread, topped with stuff), from oozing cheesy bread to banana and chocolate topped, erm, bread. Not exactly Atkins friendly, but then again he's dead. So who really cares?

snack....

party...

Nowhere more so than in Dubai's clubs is it obvious that this is a place with money. And money that it is more than happy to spend on Champagne. Moreover, nowhere is it less apparent that this is, after all, a Muslim country – at the most glittering end of the scale, the hotpant and wonderbra brigade are wall-to-wall. Not that the leggy lovelies who frequent most venues need to be bought tipples – it is another peculiarity of the nightlife scene that free drinks for ladies are *de rigueur*, even in the swankiest of dens of iniquity, at least once a week.

As there are surprisingly few clubs of any real repute, doormen at some venues can afford to be choosy and can be decided surly. Others won't even entertain the thought of your entrance if you haven't booked a table. It is pretty egalitarian if you can be bothered to plan your night in advance – but some require a hefty minimum spent to take a table. The plush, red-and-gold 400 Club is one such venue, and 360°, as it's almost as much of a tourist attraction as the Burj Al Arab that it stands next door to, is Fort Knox in a Friday night. If you want to witness some serious cash being splashed, Plastik – which has its own beach, yacht moorings and a helipad – styles itself as pure St Tropez and the name is particularly apt given the clientele.

Some of the larger clubs – Chi at the Lodge being the big kid on the block – do attract household name DJs (one of the most famous, Grooverider, managing to get himself jailed for possession of drugs on his way to a set there). It's worth re-iterating that drugs, in any form, carry a minimum term of four years, no questions asked. Which is probably a big reason that Dubai is not big on all-night raves – very rarely will a venue open past the 3am mark. Still, big promoters like Hed Kandi and the Hat Club do put on the occasional night.

If you're happy to step outside the five-star comfort zone, the sort of hotels you probably wouldn't dream of checking into house some insider clubs – Café Filipino Maharlika is one of the friendliest and best, and many boast brilliant house covers bands. Live music apart from that can be difficult to find, although The Irish Village and Malecon sometimes have a decent selection.

There are no brothels in the city and prostitution is illegal. There are also no openly gay venues as it's very much frowned upon, although again keep an ear to the ground and it might be possible to find one that leans that way.

360° *(bottom)*
Jumeirah Beach Hotel, Jumeirah
Tel: 04 406 8769
www.jumeirahbeachhotel.com
Open: daily, 5pm–2am

Sitting pretty on its own pier out in the Gulf Sea and overlooked by the ludicrously huge Burj Al Arab hotel, it's no wonder that 360° has become the go-to place for sundowner drinking sessions. This means, however, that the place soon fills up, and unless you're there for early doors – or think ahead and book a table – you'll most likely find yourself having to queue while the burly bouncers operate a one-in-one-out policy (and check your ID). It's worth it, though, for the view. And if sipping *mojitos* while the blazing sun slips into the distant horizon sounds a little pedestrian to your ears then worry not – as the night progresses, the pretty, pampered punters tend to drift away from the circular central bar and onto the, er, 'compact' dancefloor.

The 400 Club *(right)*
Fairmont Hotel, Sheikh Zayed Road
Tel: 04 332 4900
www.the400nightclub.com
Open: Tuesday, Thursday and Friday 10pm–3am

Exclusive and proud of it, The 400 Club operates a strict couples-only and smart clothing policy to keep out the riff-raff. Get past the unapologetic bouncers, though, and you'll find one of the plushest clubbing venues in the city – though it's not the biggest, so expect to be literally rubbing shoulders with the city's beautiful people if you feel like dancing. The club attracts a large Lebanese quotient, so expect concessions to Lebanese music tastes, but there are usually plenty of chart and classic tunes on offer as well. If you do decide to frequent the place then it's not a bad idea to sign up to their membership scheme, as they will on occasion get some big names in to give invite-only gigs.

Alpha *(left)*
Le Méridien Dubai, Garhoud
Tel: 04 217 0000
dubai.lemeridien.com
Open: daily, 9pm–3am

One of the newest big boys on the nightlife scene, Alpha is also one of the few that is actually run by nightclub managers as opposed to hotel managers. And that means a good selection of music from breaks to indie, not to mention the occasional live international band. It tends to attract a cool, largely female crowd, with plenty of artists, journos and designers in the mix. All of this is thankfully enough to distract from the size of the venue (it's massive, having been converted from a cavernous Greek restaurant rather than built to order). During the winter, the balcony is also opened up for some *al fresco* dancing, with a huge glass window letting clubbers keep an eye on the dance floor below, and take in the unique Greco-Roman architecture.

The Apartment *(left)*
Jumeirah Beach Hotel, Jumeirah
Tel: 04 406 8000
Open: 5pm–3am Tues–Sat

This basement club has been through several incarnations – including one as a French fine dining restaurant – but thankfully it has returned to its roots as a cosy and exclusive after-dark hang-out. Its eclectic music policy – and a raft of big name DJs passing through – means it's hard to pin down the clientele, but it keeps drawing in the punters despite an occasionally difficult door policy (early arrival or booking is recommended at the weekend). In keeping with the elitist theme, there's an above average selection of wines and cocktails and a competent kitchen. The dressed up crowd can be slow to take to the mirrored dance floor, but to be fair it is hard to drag yourself away from the deep sofas in the lounge area, where you can ogle the beautiful people ogling themselves in the enormous mirrors.

Boudoir *(right)*
Dubai Marine Beach Resort and Spa, Jumeirah
Tel:04 345 5995
www.myboudoir.com
Open: daily, 7.30pm–3am

With the tagline, "Wild luxury, extreme opulence", from the minute you step into Boudoir it's completely obviously what sort of joint this is. And, if you were in any doubt, the fact the music cuts out when the big spenders order their obelisk-sized jeroboams will set your mind at rest. Red velvet, shining gilt and more drapes than, erm, a tart's boudoir, it's opulence-by-numbers, but still manages to pack in the crowds to its numerous theme rooms every night. It's also a haven for the poor-but-beautiful – Tuesdays and Thursdays see it jam-packed with perky girls, lured by the free Champage or cocktails. The music is never particularly challenging, but happy house, r'n'b and pop tunes are all sprinkled into the mix, and are enough to get the largely Lebanese and French crowd going.

Cavalli Club *(bottom)*
Fairmont Dubai, Sheikh Zayed Road
Tel: 04 332 9260
www.cavalliclubdubai.com
Open: daily, 7.30pm–2am

Want to eat gold? Yes, actual gold. Get thee to the Cavalli Club then. Not that designer Roberto Cavalli himself could ever be accused of subtlety, but this sort of bling – cranked up to eleven, gold leafed, and then doused liberally in Cristal – has to be seen to be believed. The unprepossessing entrance at the back of the Fairmont Hotel gives little of the game away, but as you ascend the black marble stairs that seem designed to break your ankle (seriously, it's pitch black – girls, take your heels off or get a piggyback), you get an inkling of what awaits. At the top, you'll find a cavernous space literally dripping in Swarovski from a ballroom-height ceiling. Primarily a restaurant at the beginning of the night, the main dining area – where you can eat the aforementioned gold, in a signature sushi dish that also includes Wagyu,

party...

127

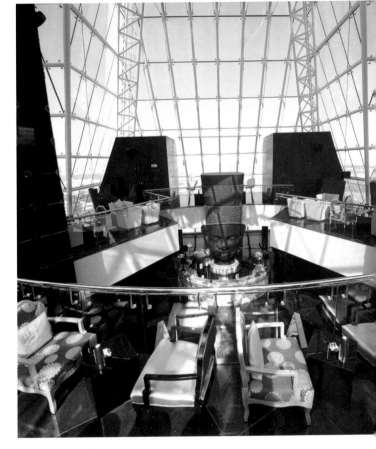

caviar and lobster, or more standard Italian fare – is the focus of the space early on, but as the night proceeds, glammed-up guests disperse to the various elevated VIP pods to dance under the dramatically suspended DJ booth until it's time to hit the 400 Club, round the corner, at 2am. If you can make it down the stairs in one piece.

....

Chi At The Lodge *(left)*
Al Nasr Leisureland, Garhoud
Tel: 04 337 9470
www.lodgedubai.com
Open: 9pm–3am. Closed Fridays.

Something of a Dubai legend, this is the biggest – and undoubtedly the most popular – club in the city. Located in the run-down and grubby Al Nasr Leisureland complex – complete with ice rink and crap rides – the interior of Chi is infinitely more pleasurable, featuring four different bar/club sections: poky Chi Red, no-nonsense Chi Club, plush Chi Lounge and the massive Chi Garden arena. It attracts everyone from the posh to the proles, but if you're in a big group and want a big, unpretentious night out then you'd be hard pushed to do better. Friday nights feature four different genres of music, with a headline act taking the Chi Garden stage. Meanwhile, midweek events tend to focus on special parties and guest appearances, with previous acts ranging from Grammy-winning hip hop act De La Soul to celebrated folk musician José González.

....

China Moon *(bottom)*
Raffles Dubai,
Sheikh Rashid Road
Tel: 04 314 9888 www.raffles.com
Open: daily, 7pm–3am

You would have thought that a location at the apex of Raffles' glass-walled pyramid would have instantly secured this sleek, slick bar a spot at the top of the nightlife list, but in truth its 'attitude with altitude' took a while to get going. Initially, the terrier-like doormen stopped anyone who looked like they might not want to drop a week's wages on a bottle of Cristal getting up the shiny black stairs, but a more lax approach – and the addition of the city's best promoters – and it's now the place to pout and be pouted at come the weekend. The music is eclectic – from happy house to eighties cheese, and the wall-to-wall punters impeccably dressed. It still attracts a seriously moneyed, older crowd though, hanging out by the pyramid's glass walls – and we mean that literally – in the retro sixties pod chairs suspended from the ceiling.

....

The Irish Village *(right)*
Tel: 04 282 4750
www.theirishvillage.ae
Open: daily, 11am–1.15am
(2.15am Weds/Thurs)

Strictly speaking, this gargantuan hooch hole is actually an Irish pub – or at least the sort of approximation of one you might expect from someone who had never set foot on the Emerald Isle. But the late license, an embarrassment of outdoor space and the fact that there is no hotel to keep awake within holler-

party...

ing distance means that it's also made a name for itself as prime venue to listen to live acts. Even during the sweltering summer months, the terrace area, which wraps around an enormous duck pond, packs in the crowds to sit on the rickety wooden benches and soak up the sounds of everyone from Clannad to The Stranglers and a pint of Kilkenny. Once a year, it also holds Hopfest, a celebration of the brown stuff, with live bands and more beers that you could shake a trouser leg at.

JamBase *(left)*
Souk Madinat Jumeirah, Jumeirah
Tel: 04 366 6730
www.madinatjumeirah.com
Open: daily, 7pm–2am

Branded as a 'supper club', JamBase really stands out as a nightclub venue. As the dark draws in, this venue comes alive with the sound of funk, pop and soul, courtesy of its rather good resident band. Get in there early, though, because the astonishing popularity of this place means that you'll almost certainly have to queue for ages beforehand, and subsequently finding a table in the amassed dancers, drinkers and party animals can be next-to-impossible. And the bar never seems to have quite enough staff to manage either. Still, with some of the most bouncy, fun music in town, this dressed-down venue can be a real stormer. And being in the Souk Madinat, should you decide to stretch your legs and head off somewhere less crowded, you'll find plenty to do.

Maharlika Café Filipino *(right)*
The President Hotel, Bur Dubai
Open: 04 344 6565
Tel: daily, 6pm–3am

Take the lift up to the fourth floor of the distinctly dodgy-looking President Hotel in the definitely unfashionable Bur Dubai area and you are faced with two choices – right for the Indian Club and left for the Filipino club. Both do exactly what they say on the tin, but the latter benefits from the best covers band in the whole world. Ever. Seriously – send a request to the front on a napkin and you can convince them to do anything from Bon Jovi to Beyonce. In between the chart pop and golden oldies spun by the unashamedly mainstream DJ, the entire population of the dark, low-ceilinged room (who are 98% Filipino – no false promises here) take their seats at the edges of the dance floor, all the better to appreciate the gymnastic gyrations of the excitable backing dancers. An antidote to the self-conscious stylings of Dubai's see-and-be-seen clubs, it's an just a brilliantly fun night out.

Malecon *(bottom)*
Dubai Marine Beach Resort And Spa, Jumeirah
Tel: 04 346 1111
www.dxbmarine.com/malecon.php
Open: daily, 7pm–3am

If you're a little tired of the polished and pretty clubs of Dubai, then head over to this Cuban-themed bar, whose walls, chairs and tables are covered with miles of graffiti and hand-scrawled messages. Far from looking grubby,

however, it only adds to the exotic ambience, as does the Latin music. And if you're looking for something to do on a Sunday night, then it's worth checking out their salsa nights for beginners and intermediates, which attract a wide cross-section of Dubai's expat culture. Otherwise, you can just sink into one of the gloriously soft and plush leather sofas, buy yourself a Cuban cigar and enjoy the closest thing you'll get to Cuba without having to leave the country. And when you're done, you can wander out back and take in the rushing tide, which runs right up to the back of the hotel.

Plan B *(top)*
Wafi, Garhoud
Tel: 04 324 4777 www.wafi.com
Open: daily, 7pm–1am (2am Tues–Fri)

Located in the ludicrous faux-Egyptian Wafi mall, just next to Planet Hollywood, Plan B is popular with the younger residents of Dubai and puts on a whole swathe of internationally branded clubbing nights, as well as some homegrown ones. Built on two levels with a smaller bar overlooking the main floor, it may not be the biggest of clubs but it certainly does a lot with what it has, and is invariably packed out with up-for-it clubbers. And they have to be up for it, too, because once you're inside Plan B there's no escaping the (predominantly house) music. Instead, it's best to weave on into the dancefloor and get your body moving.

Plastik *(middle)*
Golden Tulip Al Jazira, Ghantoot
(between Dubai and Abu Dhabi)
Tel: 02 562 9100
www.plastikbeach.com
Open: daily, times vary

A club for people with more money than sense (and body fat), Plastik is actually a gorgeous venue if you are prepared to smile at the nouveau-riche stylings of its owners. With a helicopter pad, moorings for yachts and a multi-tiered system that segregates the big spenders from the slightly-less-big-spenders, it's not one for the Socialists among you. But frankly, those on the swanky, rich-people-only sections are missing out on the real fun: the Jacuzzis. Nothing says Dubai like smoking *shisha* from a Jacuzzi while sipping a cocktail! As well as operating like a nightclub, the venue is also open earlier in the day as a restaurant and (occasionally) spa, so if you plan ahead you can get a good day's fun out of it. Which you'll have to, because it's a good few miles outside of Dubai itself.

Soluna *(bottom)*
Layali Tent, Mina A'Salam Hotel, Jumeirah
Tel: 04 366 8888
www.madinatjumeirah.com
Open: 6am–11pm Saturday

This is a curious one and no mistake: six nights a week, Soluna is actually 'Layali Tent', a massive tent-based restaurant. But every Saturday it transforms into Soluna, a beach-side bar that overlooks both the Gulf Sea and the Burj Al Arab

hotel (and is therefore the direct competitor of Dubai favourite 360°). This cool sundown spot plays chilled beats while throngs of happy – and often rather pretty – punters pack out the bars. Be forewarned, though: there's a minimum spend on tables and you have to book them ahead of time; call the hotel for more info. There's also a no-sportswear clothing policy. In the summertime the intense heat drives Soluna into the air-conditioned tent, but frankly without the sand between your toes it's a little bit pointless.

Submarine *(top)*
The Dhow Palace, Bur Dubai
Tel: 04 359 9992
www.dhowpalacedubai.com
Open: daily, 6pm–3am

If you want a taste of Dubai's underground – literally – then wander on down to Submarine, located beneath The Dhow Palace Hotel in the nitty-gritty Bur Dubai district. It won't win any awards for glamour, but this dark and quirky venue does have an odd charm – make sure you go there late on, however, as it doesn't generally pick up steam until around midnight. It's worth checking ahead about the music policy, too, because the management have become notorious for changing the various nights regularly, particularly in an attempt to shake the club's reputation for being the focal point for Dubai's gay community (the UAE's policy on homosexuality – it's legal, but gay acts aren't – makes such venues jumpy). Consequently, it's building up a following in the city's Filipino and rock music cliques too.

Warehouse *(bottom)*
Le Meridien Dubai, Garhoud
Open: daily, 6pm–3am, Friday 1pm–3am, Saturday/Sunday 6pm–3am
Tel: 04 217 0000

To call the Warehouse a club is a bit unfair – this behemoth of a nightspot boasts more venues than your average suburban city centre, and surprisingly, it manages to be all things to all people. The biggest draw is the nightclub, which sits on the first floor and, at weekends sees big-name DJs playing to a high-spirited ex-pat crowd. If you plan to spend all evening here, you could do worse than holing up in the beer garden below, or hunkering down in the bare brick-walled wine lounge next to it, which boasts its own impressive cheese room. Upstairs, and Asian fusion restaurant offers less relaxed dining, with white-draped loungers on a terrace overlooking the airport (well, you can't have everything) to enjoy a cocktail and a cigar before cutting up the small but perfectly-formed dance floor. A word of warning – on Fridays, the venue holds an all-you-can-eat (and drink) brunch, so by nightfall, you might see some very interesting shapes being thrown.

culture...

In its mad dash to the future, Dubai nearly forgot it had a past. The rediscovery of its Arabic and Bedouin roots has led to huge investment in preserving the region's unique artistic and cultural heritage.

One of the most successful preservation areas is Bastakiya, on the Creek in Bur Dubai. It was settled in the early 1900s by traders from Bastak in southern Iran (hence its name) and is one of Dubai's few pedestrian areas, devoted to culture and tradition. Along its winding, cobbled alleyways you'll find a fascinating place where 100-year old wind towers (*barjeels*) rise above galleries showing the latest modern art. Dubai's history as a trading port has led to a rich blend of cultures all adding their own flavours to the mix. For hundreds of years, India, Iran, and Northern Africa have been sending their goods-laden *dhows* to Dubai, and if you stroll along the waterside you can still watch them sailing up the Creek.

In the UAE, Arabs have a deep respect for learning and culture. Folklore, poetry, crafts and music are all popular expressions of the aesthetic sensibility – even HH Sheikh Mohammed is an accomplished poet (you can even read some of his poems in translation at www.sheikhmohamed.com). Ancient Arabic pastimes such as falconry, horsemanship, and camel racing are still as popular as the latest football match, while traditional Bedouin crafts like weaving reveal a flair for the decorative that resonates throughout Dubai.

Family life plays a paramount role in Emirati society. The conservative and highly structured hierarchy of relationships creates strong bonds that evolve over generations. Respect for elders, loyalty to the clan, and living honourably in accordance with Islamic principles are at the heart of society. Family events like weddings are huge celebrations that can last for more than a week. Although on the surface Dubai Arabs can appear quite westernised, you'll find that old traditions are alive and well, one of the most popular being the hospitable tradition of sharing coffee.

The call to prayer from the towers of one of Dubai's beautiful mosques serves as a reminder that religion is woven in to the fabric of daily life much more than in the west. Although Islam is the official religion, Dubai welcomes people of different faiths – Dubai has always been open to other cultures as part of its trading heritage.

Now more than ever, Dubai is attracting creative talent from across the Arab world, India and Turkey, making this an exciting time for emerging artists. Political and economic problems in other Middle Eastern countries have resulted in artists seeking refuge in Dubai's stability, strong economy and creative atmosphere. The result is that Dubai today is much more than a repository of past treasures – it is the epicentre of the flourishing contemporary Middle Eastern art scene. Auction houses like Christie's and Bonham's recently launched in Dubai and set new records for Middle Eastern contemporary art. Artists like Iranian sculptor Parviz Tanavoli, who could barely make a living at home, had one of his pieces sell for $2.8 million at Christie's.

The massive warehouses of Al Quoz are where the action is, with a cluster of cutting-edge galleries. Don't be put off by its location (off Sheikh Zayed Rd behind the Times Square shopping mall) – once you get past the ugly industrial exteriors, it's a fabulous space. The Dubai International Finance Centre, once a stodgy banker zone, has become an exciting new enclave for galleries like Opera and ArtSpace. The fledgling Art Dubai fair held in March (www.artdubai.ae) has attracted a global following.

The performing arts are now very much a part of the scene. One of Dubai's most eagerly awaited projects is the stunning 2,500-seat opera house designed by über architect Zaha Hadid, in the shape of a futuristic sand dune, while the renowned Cirque du Soleil is soon to have its own theatre on The Palm.

Live entertainment has taken off – with everyone from Kylie to Jose Carreras coming to town. Music festivals like Desert Rock (www.desertrockfestival.com) and Desert Rhythm have brought out Sting, Whitney Houston, Elton John, Robbie Williams and Mika to play for sell out crowds. Dubai even has its own hot rock band, Abri. Outdoor events like the innovative and popular Peanut Butter Jam, on the Rooftop Gardens at Wafi City has locals and visitors alike perched on bean-bags and eating barbecue while listening to live music.

Movie buffs will enjoy the Dubai International Film Festival (www.dubaifilmfest.com) a starry annual event (recent celebs include George Clooney and Oliver Stone) that provides a chance to see international and Middle Eastern independent filmmakers in action.

One of the great myths about Dubai is that it lacks soul or culture – that it's all sunshine and shopping. Once you explore Dubai's energetic, inspiring cultural scene you'll see why it's becoming one of the most creative places on the planet.

Museums and places of cultural importance

Dubai has a small selection of excellent museums and cultural institutions. For a more in-depth study of regional traditional arts visit the museums and galleries in Sharjah, a small emirate known for its artistic tradition, just under an hour from Dubai. The Sharjah Islamic Museum (www.sharjahtourism.ae) is one of the best in the region.

Al Ahmadiya School

Al Ahmadiya St,
(behind Heritage House) Deira
Tel: 04 226 0286
www.dubaitourism.ae
Open: daily, 8am (2.30pm Fri)–
7.30pm

Founded in 1912, this modest school has educated many of Dubai' s most illustrious residents, including HH Sheikh Mohammed. Now a museum, it provides a fascinating glimpse into Emirati life before the oil boom, with wonderful old photos and rare video footage. To step into the beautifully restored classroom is like going back in time, and helps visitors understand the educational achievements of this Dubai institution.

Dubai Museum

Bur Dubai
Tel: 04 353 1862
www.dubaitourism.ae
Open: daily, 8.30am (2.30pm Fri)–
8.30pm

Located in historic Al Fahidi Fort, built in 1787 and Dubai's oldest major building, is one of the most popular cultural destinations for visitors wanting to delve into Dubai's past and rags-to-riches history. Galleries recreate scenes from the Creek, traditional Arab houses, mosques, the souk, date farms, desert and marine life, with one of the best exhibits portraying pearl diving, complete with sets of pearl merchants' weights, scales and sieves. With its life-size mannequins and dioramas, it's a bit 'Madame Tussauds goes to Dubai', but highly informative nevertheless.

Heritage & Diving Village

Al Shindagha, Deira
Tel: 04 393 7151
www.dubaitourism.ae
Open: daily, 8am–10pm
(8–11am and 4–10pm Fri)

Explore this fascinating 'living museum' in the newly restored Shindagha heritage area along the Creek, where you can watch craftspeople at work as well as learn about Dubai's maritime history as a centre of the pearl industry. Displays include potters and weavers practicing their crafts, as well as exhibits and demonstrations of pearl diving. During the weekend evenings there are often dance and music displays, as well as camel rides and souvenir stands where visitors can purchase local crafts. Try the freshly-made local fried donuts – a favourite Emirati snack.

Heritage House

Al Ahmadiya St, Deira
Tel: 04 226 0286
www.dubaitourism.ae
Open: daily, 8am (2.30pm Fri)–
7.30pm

Beautifully restored, this house built in 1890 was later the home of one of Dubai's great merchant princes, Sheikh Mohammed bin Ahmed bin Dalmouk, who was top of the pearl trade. An elegant example of an upper class mansion in traditional Emirati style, with a luxurious *majlis* (reception room) featuring Persian carpets and rich textiles, high walls and a sandy courtyard, the house includes a variety of lovingly restored rooms, like the charming Bride's quarters. If you want to see how people lived in Dubai before the age of the high rise, Heritage House is the perfect place to wander through. Don't miss the historic Al Ahmadiya School next door.

Jumeira Mosque

Jumeirah Beach Rd, Jumeirah
Tel: 04 353 6666

Although not generally open to the public unless you book a tour in advance, this beautiful mosque is one of Dubai's best-known and loved landmarks. The hour-long tours are on Sat, Sun, Tues and Thurs at 10am prompt. Afterwards there is a question and answer period with the expert guides who show you around. No shorts or sleeveless tops permitted, shoes must be removed and women must cover their heads. Luckily cameras are allowed so visitors can capture the delicate Islamic decoration.

Khan Murjan Gallery

Wafi
www.wafi.com
Open daily, 10am–10pm
(midnight Thurs/Fri)

Strange to think that the inside of a 21st century shopping mall one could discover a fully realised reproduction of a 14th century Arabian souk, but in Dubai's surreal world anything is possible. See traditional artisans from throughout the Middle East at work and indulge your imagination as you drift pass the traditional shops selling everything from Lebanese hand made soaps to Jordanian brass coffee pots and Persian carpets in rainbow colours. A real Aladdin's cave and great fun to visit for total immersion in Arabian crafts. The atmospheric courtyard restaurant serves excellent regional cuisine, and there's often music in the evening.

Sheikh Mohammed Centre for Cultural Understanding

Bastikiya
Tel 04 353 6666 www.cultures.ae

Tucked away in the cobbled lanes of the Bastikiya preservation area, the centre is worth popping by if you are in the area. Devoted to fostering understanding of the traditions and customs of the UAE, it offers such valuable activities as tours of the Jumeirah Mosque, and a brilliant weekly coffee morning where visitors can meet and chat with UAE nationals about their culture, with some fascinating results.

Sheikh Saeed Al Maktoum House

Shindiga Bur Dubai
Tel: 04 393 7139
www.dubaitourism.ae
Open: daily, 8.30am–9pm
Sat–Thurs; 3.30–9.30pm Fri

The home of Dubai's legendary ruler, from 1912–58, and grandfather of the present ruler has been painstakingly restored to its former glory: an example of traditional Emirati architecture, with walls made from crushed local coral, lime and plaster. The highlight of the museum is the rare and wonderful collection of historic photographs revealing Dubai in her infancy. It's almost impossible to believe the cluster of palm frond huts and fishing boats on the beach was all that existed in Jumeirah only a generation ago. Head to the upper rooftop for its scenic views along the Creek, and if you're hungry and up for a bit of local colour, pop into Kan Zaman, a popular local restaurant – big, bustling and totally authentic, at prices a fraction of your five-star.

Galleries

With so many galleries opening it's impossible to list them all, but this is a selection of interesting Dubai galleries with a proven track record and a genuine interest in promoting the region's art. For a comprehensive listing of galleries, visit www.artinthecity.com. Opening times can vary, especially during Ramadan, so check before you arrive.

B21 Art Gallery

Al Quoz 3, Off Sheikh Zayed Rd. at Interchange 3
Tel: 04 340 3965
www.b21artgallery.com

Provocative and innovative, B21 goes boldly where other galleries fear to tread. The gallery is a hotbed of young artists, often holding their first-time solo exhibitions. B21 has been open since 2005 and represents contemporary artists from all over the Middle East.

Green Art Gallery

51st Street, Villa # 23, Jumeirah, (just off Beach Rd)
Tel: 04 344 9888 www.gagallery.com

This attractive villa, now home to one of Dubai's leading galleries, is a perfect place to escape for a bit of culture after too much mall and beach action. Inside, the airy, high-ceilinged rooms feature exhibitions of artists throughout the region. The owners have launched a variety of artists who have since become well known, so it's a good place to discover up-and-coming talent. Open October to May.

Majlis Gallery

Bastakiya, Bur Dubai
Tel: 04 353 6233
www.majlisgallery.com

Majlis, Arabic for salon, is a charming, well-established gallery in a converted traditional house. As one of the first galleries in the area, it helped put Bastakiya on the map for art lovers. Within its whitewashed rooms, connected by a pretty courtyard garden, you'll find fine art (with desert landscapes prevailing), as well as handcrafted pottery, glass and unusual souvenirs.

Meem Gallery
Umm Suqeim Road, Jumeirah
Tel: 04 347 7883 www.meem.ae

This stunning gallery has already earned a reputation for the finest Arabic calligraphy in the region, from modern masters like Iraq's Taha Al-Hiti to rare masterpieces of ancient Islamic art. Meem has major exhibitions of the world's leading contemporary Arabic artists, like Ali Omar Ermes, whose work is collected by museums such as the Tate Modern in London.

The Third Line
Al Quoz 3, off Sheikh Zayed Rd
Tel: 04 341 1357
www.thethirdline.com

Cutting edge, multi-faceted gallery dedicated to the advancement and promotion of contemporary Middle Eastern art and culture. As well as staging regular exhibitions representing artists from throughout the Middle East, it also hosts the Arab Film Series and bi-monthly Arab Literature Circle.

Total Arts at The Courtyard
Al Quoz, off Sheikh Zayed Rd
Tel: 04 347 5050
www.courtyard-uae.com

One of the biggest and best of Dubai's new-wave galleries focusing on new Middle Eastern talent, Total Arts occupies two floors in a dramatic space able to handle futuristic art installations as well as more traditional art works. There's always something exciting happening here and the gallery is one of the buzziest in town. The Café is a hip hangout for neo-bohemians.

XVA Gallery
Bastikiya, Bur Dubai
Tel: 04 353 5383
www.xvagallery.com

Since intrepid, Middle Eastern art-loving expat Mona Hauser launched XVA (named after its house number) in 2003 it has become one of Dubai's most loved cultural destinations and a catalyst for the arts movement in Dubai. XVA promotes and inspires the work of regional and international artists. Top artists exhibited include Moussa Tiba, Farideh Lashai, Halim Al Karim, and Nadim Karam. The gallery is housed in a delightful restored merchant's house, with its own windtower and shady courtyard – artists often use the gallery as an atelier and stay, the result being the cool boutique hotel now attached. There's also an excellent café (Gordon Ramsay is a fan) and eclectic gift shop.

Theatres & Performing Arts

Dubai doesn't have a theatrical tradition like the West End or Broadway, so it has taken time for the concept to develop. But things are beginning to move, and the city has played host to world-class productions, from The Nutcracker to Madame Butterfly.

Dubai Community Theatre & Arts Centre (DUCTAC)

Mall of the Emirates, Jumeirah
Tel: 04 351 3400
www.dubaitheatre.org

This large and lively new cultural complex within the bustling Mall of the Emirates has two state of the art theatres, as well as exhibition halls, a library, and café. There is always a variety of entertainment, including opera, drama, comedy and classical music. Call or check website for performance schedule.

Madinat Theatre

Souk Madinat Jumeirah
Tel: 04 366 8888
www.madinattheatre.com

This stunning theatre has established itself as a firm favourite with Dubai's pleasure-seeking locals thanks to its elegant, intimate atmosphere and wonderful array of entertainment. With seating for less than 500, there's not a bad seat in the house. Performances include jazz musicians, stand up comics, ballet and modern dance, singers and magicians.

Jumana: Secret of the Desert

Al Sahra Desert Resort, Dubailand
Tel: 04 367 9500 www.alsahra.com

Hugely successful all singing, all-dancing Arabian folklore spectacular based on the tale of Prince Omar's search for his princess, with a cast of 60 actors, dancers, acrobats, camels & horses in a magical setting in the desert. The show features state of the art lasers, pyrotechnics, water-projected imagery, and dazzling fireworks all set to music - there's nothing else like it in the region. You can stay the night at the Al Sahra Desert Resort after the show, or dine pre- or post- theatre in one of their restaurants.

Cinemas

Dubaians are movie mad, and going to the cinema is very popular. However it's mostly mainstream films, a rare exception being during the Dubai International Film Festival when independent producers showcase their works. Beware of the prevailing arctic air conditioning and the tendency of the enthusiastic local crowd to chat on mobiles and munch snacks throughout the film. Cinemas in Dubai are seriously state of the art and some, like the cushy Cinestar at Mall of the Emirates, have 'Gold Class' screenings with seating in leather couches and waiter service. Tickets average around AED 30.

Grand Megaplex

Ibn Battuta Shopping Mall, Jumeira
Tel: 04 366 9898
www.grandcinemas.com

With 21 screens, including Dubai's first IMAX, this is one of the biggest cinema complexes in the region, showing everything from Hollywood hits to Bollywood blockbusters. Located in one of Dubai's most attractive malls, there's plenty to do before and after the film.

Grand Cineplex
Wafi City
Tel: 04 324 2000
www.grandcinemas.com

Next to the stunning, upmarket Wafi City shopping mall, this 16-screen venue for the excellent places nearby for a drink or dinner, either in the mall or at chic new hotel Raffles just across the street.

Cinestar
Mall of the Emirates, Jumeirah
Tel: 04 341 4222
www.cinestarcinemas.com

The cinema of choice for Jumeirah's gilded youth. It's good for people watching and excellent if you don't want to shop the mall – you can hide out seeing the latest hit while the others shop 'til they drop. 'Gold Class' screenings are worth checking out for the ultimate in movie-going.

Movies Under the Stars
Wafi City
Tel: 04 324 4100

The balmy Dubai nights make it easy to watch films *al fresco*. This outdoor screening venue in a delightful setting overlooking Dubai is a local favourite. Call for details or check listings in Time Out Dubai as programme schedule varies.

Event Information and Tickets

For listings and ticket information read or visit Time Out Dubai (www.timeout-dubai.com) or What's On. The Time Out Ticket Line sells tickets for events (tel: 800 4669; www.itp.net/tickets).

Alternatively, your hotel Concierge should be able to set you up. Prices for concerts and other events are refreshingly lower than you'd pay in the UK, so it's worth checking out what's on when you visit.

culture…

shop…

Dubai loves to shop. It may be giving slightly too much credit to cultural memory, but Dubai's acquisition obsession might have something to do with its history as a small trading port, based around the mouth of the – now vastly elongated – Creek. However it started, it's certainly true now that the malls serve the sort of function that a park or town square might in a country where it's not too hot to be outside for at least fifty percent of the time. There are even mall-walking groups that pootle around their walkways for exercise of an evening, keeping fit whilst window-shopping – pain and gain, one might say.

Open very early to very late, in the biggest malls (they are all pretty big, but some are the size of small villages) you could happily spend 24 hours flitting from restaurant to shop to ice rink to bar to bed – nearly all have hotels attached. The Mall of the Emirates was, until recently, the star shopping attraction of the Emirate, with its real snow ski slope and thousands of shoppers sticking round until its midnight closing time. But it has now been overtaken by the equally ludicrous Dubai Mall (quite literal, the Emiratis), which boasts 'the world's largest acrylic panel', behind which are 33,000 fish. Oh, and 1,200 shops. Don't expect many, if any, local stores in these monoliths, but almost every major retail player is represented. From Chanel and Louis Vuitton to Topshop and Forever 21, they are all here – French, Italian, Australian, British and American mega brands winning the minds and wallets of a nation that takes it shopping very seriously indeed.

If niche and quirky are more your thing, and you don't mind wading through a bit of tat, Bur Dubai is an interesting experience. Wander the streets near the Creek and antiques stalls selling tarnished silver jewellery, carpets and reams of fabrics abound. Karama too has its own charm and if you prefer your Chanel off the back of a truck, you'll be in heaven. Gold, a local obsession, is sold in the traditional souk in Deira, and there are certainly bargains to be had, but shop around and remember to haggle.

shop....

Bur Dubai

This bustling area is one of the few places to pound the pavements and shop in the open air. Although not quite the Arabia of old, you receive a sense of what this turn of the century fishing port was once like, as you aren't actually far from the historical hub. The area between the Dubai Museum and the Creek is packed with tiny shops – selling everything from Burj Al Arab Snowdomes to Burqa-clad Russian dolls and alarm clocks that wake you with the call to prayer – their wares spilling out onto the streets. There are also lots of hole-in-the wall stores with high-quality fabrics, imported mainly from India, piles of cheap cotton holiday gear and bejeweled flip-flops. Haggling is *de rigeur*, but unaggressive.

 Burjuman Mall
www.burjuman.com
Open: daily, 10am–10pm

As compact as serious malls get in Dubai, this is a nice place to potter round for an afternoon, with proper restaurants on the third floor (The Noodle House is always packed), and prices that ascend as you do, floor by floor, until you reach Chanel and Prada at the very top. The only downside is that the queue for a taxi post-splurge is heart-attack inducing. Sneak round the back and you'll hail one instantly. Stores include:

Baume & Mercier, Burberry, Calvin Klein, Canali, Cartier, Celine, Chaumet, Christian Dior, Christian Lacroix, D&G, Diesel, DKNY, Dolce & Gabbana, Donna Karan, Escada, Etro, Fendi, Gianfranco Ferre, Hermes, Just Cavalli, Kenzo, La Perla, Lacoste, Levi's, Longchamp, Louis Vuitton, Magrudy's, Marina Rinaldi, Mont Blanc, Paul & Shark, Paul Smith, Polo Ralph Lauren, Prada, Saks Fifth Avenue, Salvatore Ferragamo, Samsonite, Shanghai Tang, Sonia Rykiel, TAG Heuer, Tod's, Valentino, Versace, Vertu, Virgin Megastore and Zara.

 Dubai Festival City
Airport Road
www.festivalcentre.com

Gargantuan mall with Dubai's only Ikea and the enormous Hyper Panda supermarket – a great place to stock up on dates, *halva* and *baklava* to take home. There's also an outdoor promenade with coffee shops and restaurants when you need to take the weight of tired feet. Stores include:

Accessorize, Bose, Bugatti, Camper, Carolina Herrera, Converse, Diesel, DKNY, Dunhill, Ed Hardy, Esprit, Fire Trap, Forever 21, Fred Perry, French Connection, Gas, Guess, Hugo Boss, Karen Millen, Kenneth Cole, Kenzo, La Senza, Lacoste, Levi's, M Missoni, Marc by Marc Jacobs, Magrudy's, Marks & Spencer, Mont Blanc, Nicky Hilton, Pal Zileri, Paul & Joe, Paul Smith, Puma, Reiss, Samsonite, Tommy Hilfiger, Tumi, Versace JC and Vilbrequin.

Dubai Mall
Downtown Bur Dubai
www.thedubaimall.com
Open: daily, 10am–midnight

The opening date of this mall was put back four times. Finally throwing its doors open at the end of 2008, it's not hard to see why, as alongside 1,200 shops, it's also got an Olympic ice rink, a cinema complex and Sega Republic indoor theme park, to name but a few of its OTT attractions. You could easily spend a day here, with the epic food court providing stodgy international sustenance (it boasts the country's only Taco Bell). It even has its own shiny approximation of a gold souk, complete with giant, glittering gold tree. The opening of Waitrose threw ex-pat Brits into a state of high excitement. Stores include:

Accessorize, Adidas Original, Adolfo Dominguez, Alberta Ferretti, Alexander McQueen, Alfred Dunhill, Armani Casa, Banana Republic, Bang & Olufsen, Birkenstock, Bloomingdales, Book World by Kinokunya, Bose, Brioni, Burberry, Canali, Canon, Carolina Herrera, Cartier, Chanel, Chloé, Chopard, Clarins, D&G, D'squared, Dean & Deluca, Diesel, Dior, Duchamp, Ed Hardy, Ermengildo Zegna, Etro, Face Stockholm, Fendi, Galaries Lafayette, Galliano, Gianfranco Ferre, Givenchy, Glitter, Graff, Gucci, Guess, H&M, Hackett, Harley Davidson, Hermes, Jaeger-LeCoultre, Jean-Paul Gaultier, Jimmy Choo, John Lobb, Joseph, K2, Karen Millen, Kenzo, Lanvin, Levi's, Loewe, Longchamp, Longines, Louis Vuitton, MAC, Magrudy's, Mandarina Duck, Manolo Blahnik, Marc by Marc Jacobs, Marks & Spencer, Matthew Williamson, Missoni, Mont Blanc, Mumbai Se, North Face, Patek Phillippe, Paul Smith, Penhaligon's, Pucci, Ralph Lauren, S*uce, Samsonite, Sephora, Stella McCartney, Swarovski, Tag Heuer, Temperley, Thomas Pink, Tom Ford, Tommy Hilfiger, Top Shop, Tumi, Valentino, Van Cleef & Arpels, Versace, Vertu, Von Dutch, Waitrose and Zara.

Gold Souk
Deira

The wares at the Deira gold market won't be to everyone's taste – the colour is much yellower than most Western eyes are used to, since the majority is actually 24 carat – but it's worth it for the experience, nonetheless. There are over 300 traders pack into a small space, selling everything from megacarat diamonds, to Sex and the City-style name necklaces, to their Arabic equivalent.

Gold & Diamond Park
Sheikh Zayed Road

A more sanitised version of the gold souk on the wrong side of the Creek, big name jewellers sit alongside smaller outlets. Haggling is encouraged, but most pure gold pieces are sold by weight at the price fixed that day, so there may be less leeway than you'd expect.

Jumeirah Beach Road

The Beach Road is dotted with mini malls and independent stores housed in pretty villas. They are frequented largely by the well-to-do families that live in the white marble houses on the beach, so expect expensive.

THE One – a huge hanger of a furniture shop with a brilliant selection of small gifts and a great café. There isn't one home in Dubai without a piece from this local chain.

The Village Mall

Sugar Daddy's – divine cupcakes to take away
Ayesha Depala – Dubai's first lady of fashion designs dream gowns, and stocks her own pick of international designers and gorgeous handmade chocolates.
S*uce – an eclectic mix of the hippest labels for girls about town
Luxecouture – laid back luxury womenswear from niche, largely American, brands

Jumeirah Centre

S*uce Lite – the discount little sister of the hip independent womenswear boutique across the road.

Mercato Mall

Red Earth – Australian cosmetics brand
Virgin Megastore – multimedia monolith selling books, CDs and DVDs

Jumeirah Emirates Towers Boulevard

www.jumeirahemiratestowers.com/lifestyle
Open: daily, 10am (4pm Fri)–10pm

The highest of high end fashion is nestled in this little mall in the financial district, all the better for the bankers to stock up on Balenciaga in their lunch breaks. Stores include:

Balenciaga, Bottega Veneta, Boucheron, Boutique 1, Bvlgari, Cartier, Chloé, Emilio Pucci, Ermenegildo Zegna, Giorgio Armani, Gucci, Jimmy Choo, Juicy Couture, Lanvin, Rodeo Drive and Yves Saint Laurent.

Karama Shopping Complex
Karama

'Copy watch! Real fake copy watch!' will come the cry as you wander round the decidedly dodgy looking, higgledy-piggledy collection of shops. The vendors are utterly unashamed of flogging fake Louis Vuitton, Chanel and Tiffany to the masses. The knock-offs can range from good to giggle-inducing, but it is a shopping experience unlike any other in Dubai, that will see you whisked into a raft of redundant back rooms to see 'the good stuff' (clearly nobody in authority cares enough to stop the openly-practiced racket, but the traders think the clandestine posturing adds to authenticity – go along with it).

Mall Of The Emirates
Sheikh Zayed Road
www.malloftheemirates.com
Open: 10am–10pm (midnight Thurs–Sat)

Permanently packed right up until its midnight closing time, this is a Dubai landmark, helped by the real snow ski slope that makes it part shopping experience, part tourist attraction. Arm yourself with a map – it's very, very easy to get lost. Stores include:

Alfred Dunhill, Asprey, B&B Italia, Bo-Concept, Biotherm, Boom & Mellow, Borders, Breitling, Bugatti, Burberry, Bvlgari, Carolina Herrera, Diesel, DKNY, Dolce & Gabbana, Emporio Armani, Etro, Gant, Gucci, Guess, H&M, Harvey Nichols, Kenneth Cole, Koton, La Perla, La Senza, Lacoste, Louis Vuitton, Marc Jacobs, Missoni, Mont Blanc, Morgan, Mothercare, Oxbow, Paul & Shark, Paul Smith, Porsche Design, Ralph Lauren, Reiss, Roberto Cavalli, Salvatore Ferragamo, Vacheron Constantin, Versace, Virgin Megastore, Whistles, Yves St Laurent and Zara.

Outlet Mall
Al Ain Road

Where last season's clothes come to die, you don't know the meaning to the word bargain until you've pitched up at this Al Ain Road outpost. Most of the major boutiques and brands have concessions here, selling serious labels at shockingly slashed prices.

Levi's – American denim at knock-down prices
Priceless – a little hit and miss and sizing is an issue (meaning, they most probably don't have yours) but spend an hour in here and you'll almost certainly unearth a gem
The Outlet – Boutique 1 offloads its wares here after they've passed their

sell-by date, but it's all in tip-top condition. Occasional 90% off sales make it credit crunch heaven
THE One – from sofas to photo frames, samples, cancelled orders and floor-damaged stock is available at hefty discounts from this furniture and accessories chain

Souk Madinat
Jumeirah

More of a retail theme park than a mall, the souk here is peppered with some fine dining options and surrounded by the Madinat's lazy waterways. Stalls are set out in front of the permanent shops with typical tourist tat – cuddly camels, piles of evil eyes (don't buy one for yourself – it's bad luck) and 'I heart Dubai' T-shirts. Kitsch and fun, but ten times cheaper in Bur Dubai.

Wafi, Dubai Creek

www.wafi.com
Open: daily, 10am–10pm (midnight Thurs/Fri)

You don't get more ridiculous than Wafi Mall. A little – well, a lot actually – of Vegas in Dubai, it is shaped like a pyramid and the entrances are flanked by sphinxes. For some inexplicable reason, it's never, ever busy, but houses a huge range of well-stocked shops. The adjoining Khan Murjan souk is gobsmacking, with it's huge stained glass windows and hundreds of small shops selling carpets, lamps and traditional (read – very, very strong) perfumes. Stores include:

shop...

Adidas, Calvin Klein, Canali, Caran d'Ache, Cerruti, Chanel, Chopard, Desert Rose, D'squared, Dunhill, Ed Hardy, Escada, Etoile, Face Stockholm, Fat Face, Frette, Gant, Gerard Darel, Ginger & Lace, Graff, Jaeger, Joop!, Kenneth Cole, La Senza, Links, Lucky Brand Jeans, MAC, Mandaria Duck, Marks & Spencer, Missoni Sport, Mont Blanc, Nicole Farhi, Patek Phillippe, Penhaligon's, Roberto Cavalli, Salam, Strenesse, Swarovski, The White Company, Topshop, Versace JC, Vertu, Villeroy & Boch, Vintage 55, and Von Dutch.

 The Walk,
Jumeirah Beach Residences

This promenade fills up at the weekend with people walking their dogs – not something you'll see often here – kids on skateboards and twenty-something groups of friends enjoying a leisurely lunch at the pavement cafes. As it's very new, shops are opening every day, but currently it still retains a flavour of independece – with any luck the enormous chains will stay away.

Boutique 1 – with a café, bookshop and gallery space, this is Dubai's first real foray into seriously chic fashion boutiques
Petit Bateau – cute-as-a-button cotton childresnwear from the French brand
Savile Row – menswear store with an in-house tailor
Zadig & Voltaire – French fashion brand with gorgeous knitwear and easy daytime pieces

Shopping List…

shop…

play...

Whether it's the beach, the sporting life, decadent nights in town or the wilds of the desert, Dubai is one of the world's great pleasure zones, so make sure you try and enjoy everything the emirate has to offer.

The saying 'work hard, play hard' could have been invented for Dubai. The emirate reflects the love of sport and outdoor life that characterises Bedouin culture and is championed by the ruling Al Maktoum family. As a result, Dubai's social scene revolves around the sporting calendar – so check ahead to see what's on. The biggest sporting events of the year are the Polo, the International Rugby Sevens, the PGA Dubai Desert Classic, the Dubai Tennis Championships, and the world's richest horse race, the Dubai World Cup (with US$6 million in prize money). As well as these sell-out events, Dubai invites overseas teams and big-name stars to play exhibition matches.

To fulfill its sporting ambitions, Dubai is building Sports City, a massive 50 million sq feet development dedicated to the active life. When completed, it will boast four stadiums, as well as an International Cricket Council Academy, Manchester United Football Academy, Butch Harmon School of Golf and a David Lloyd Tennis Academy, plus an Ernie Els 18-hole championship golf course, fitness centres and a state-of-the-art swimming complex. Sports City may be the future home of the Olympics if Dubai realises its goal of one day hosting the Games.

A little-known fact is that extreme sports are a Dubai craze. Here, you can indulge in a hair-raising variety of adrenaline rushes – skydiving, microlight flying, hot air ballooning, paragliding, power parachuting, quad biking, rock-climbing, camel racing, dune-bashing, speedboat racing, polo, and endurance riding to name but a

few. Recently two guys sneaked on to Burj Dubai, the world's tallest building and still under construction, and BASE jumped. The authorities only found out after it was posted on YouTube.

Away from the city, the desert offers outdoor adventure. Think Lawrence of Arabia and hop on a camel, or try 4x4 'dune bashing' down 100-foot slopes. Overnight safaris let you sleep under a star-filled sky in a traditional Bedouin tent, seeing the desert in all its beauty, accompanied by gazelles, Oryx, camels and falcons.

The sparkling waters of the Arabian Gulf attract watersports fans from around the world. Windsurf, wave ride and paraglide above the sea, or go diving beneath it. Whatever your favourite way to get wet, Dubai has it. Sailing has taken off, and gleaming yachts grace new marinas. Dubai's Victory powerboat racing team has been unbeatable for several years in Europe's Class 1 UIM championships.

After all that excitement, it's time to relax. Dubai has a sybaritic selection of spas, and the emirate is a holistic heaven of top treatments, luxurious surroundings, and exotic therapies, in short, everything for a top spa holiday. Why not sample a variety? Dubai is small enough that you can stay at one spa resort, and still try a tempting treatment at another. With residents from 140 countries, Dubai is one of the world's most cosmopolitan cities – good news for spa goers, with specialists and treatments from as far afield as Sweden, Thailand, India, the Philippines, Bali and more. The ancient healing benefits of Indian Ayurveda exist happily alongside the latest high-tech La Prairie facial. You'll find Arabic *rasul*, Turkish *hammam*, Greek thalassotherapy, American hot stone massage, French body wraps – only Dubai offers such a world of spa wisdom in one place.

Aerial Tours

A great way to see Dubai is from the air. Whether it's by hot air balloon, helicopter or – the latest craze – by seaplane, an aerial tour gives a unique perspective of modern Dubai.

Aerogulf Services
Dubai International Airport
Tel: 04 220 0331
www.aerogulfservices.com

Achieve Sheikh chic in your own private helicopter whizzing above the city. The four-seater choppers can fly you over all Dubai's main sights in exhilarating half- or one-hour flights, with rates starting from Dhs. 2, 925.

Balloon Adventures Dubai
Tel: 04 285 4949
www.ballooning.ae

Balloon Adventures Dubai has the largest and most advanced balloons in the UAE and offers a selection of breathtaking rides, like sunrise soaring over the red dunes of Hatta.

Seawings
Jebel Ali
Tel: 04 883 2999 www.seawings.ae

One of the newest and most amusing ways to see Dubai – this seaplane tour in a classic Cessna 208 Caravan provides a brilliant journey along Dubai's dramatic and ever changing coastal skyline. Travelling at 1,500 feet, you'll have a bird's eye view of Dubai's Downtown and iconic landmarks like The World Islands, Palm Islands, Jumeirah Beach, Dubailand, Burj Al Arab and world's tallest building, Burj Dubai.

Beyond Dubai

In 2 hours or less from Dubai's city centre, there is a world of Arabian adventure to discover. So get out of town and get into a whole different scene.

Abu Dhabi
Abu Dhabi, the UAE's oil rich capital, is Dubai's well-behaved older brother, who looks fondly at his wild child sibling but wouldn't dream of behaving like him. Abu Dhabi has an elegant Corniche ringed with fine hotels, the best being Emirates Palace, a dazzling if somewhat daunting five-star beach resort, rumoured to be the most expensive hotel ever built. The new Shangri-La resort has a lavish spa well worth making a detour for. In town, there is an impressive Cultural Foundation with various exhibitions, a working *dhow* harbour where you can see these traditional craft being made, and Heritage Village, a reproduction of a Bedouin camp complete with craftsmen, camels and falconry. Saadiyat Island is being developed into a fabulous leisure destination, with museums like the Guggenheim and the Louvre adding serious culture clout.

Al Ain
Al Ain is a desert oasis in the state of Abu Dhabi, with a lot of charm and a likeable, laid-back atmosphere. Home to the last camel market in the UAE, numerous date farms, historic forts, an excellent museum and stunning

scenery from Jebel Hafeet Mountain. The garden city, as it is known, was once a bolthole of Lawrence of Arabia and was at the crossroads of the great trading caravans. It sits at the edge of the *Rub al Khali* (Empty Quarter), where some of the world's highest sand dunes can be explored by jeep and where the great explorer Sir Wilfred Thesiger made history as the first European to cross it. The Mercure Grand Hotel (www.mercure.com) has wraparound views and is worth visiting for lunch or tea. The Hili archaeological site has artefacts from 2500 BC and is a fascinating place to explore.

Desert Safaris

The Bedouin were the trading nomads of the desert who traversed the sandy domains of Arabia for thousands of years along ancient camel routes. Although their way of life has all but disappeared, you can experience something of their culture on a desert safari. Sleep under the stars or just spend a day out and about in the incomparable desert dunes that lie just beyond Dubai's cityscape. One of Dubai's most famous dunes is 'Big Red' a popular spot for dune-bashing (riding up and down the steep inclines in a jeep, dune buggy, ATV – any vehicle that can deal with tons of sand), and sand surfing.

Dubailand

Currently under construction, this mind-boggling project located about half an hour from Downtown in what was once desert scrubland will be the most ambitious tourist destination ever created. It is colossal: its theme parks, exhibitions, leisure and entertainment facilities will make Florida's Walt Disney World Resort, currently the world's largest theme park complex, look like a children's crèche in comparison. Upon completion, Dubailand (www.dubailand.ae) will be the size of Singapore.

One of its more wacky attractions will be the Falcon City of Wonders, a recreation of the world's greatest architectural wonders infused with 21st century hi-tech features. Imagine the Pyramids, the Eiffel Tower and the Taj Mahal all in one place, all full scale and you begin to get the idea. And don't miss Restless Planet, a Jurassic Park extravaganza complete with an animated T-Rex and over a hundred other animatronic dinosaurs all built by robotics experts in Japan and costing more than a billion dollars. Also coming soon is The Great Dubai Wheel, even bigger than the London Eye. To create accommodation for the millions of visitors who are expected to visit this marvel, Dubai's government has given the green light for the Bawadi Project, nicknamed 'DuVegas', which will add a whopping 51 new hotels and 60,000 hotel rooms, including (you guessed it!) the world's biggest hotel, the 6,500 room Asia-Asia, due for completion in 2010.

Hatta

This hidden gem is the oldest village in the emirate of Dubai, nestling up against the dramatic backdrop of the Hajar Mountains. Its deep gorges and wadis are perfect for action-packed jeep safaris. Swim in the famous Hatta rock pools and laze in the shade of a date palm and have an Arabic *mezze* picnic, or enjoy lunch at the pretty Hatta Fort

Hotel, whose lush garden grounds attracts a bevy of tropical birds.

Oman's Musandam Peninsula
A stunning 2-hour drive from Dubai through the northern emirate of Ras Al Khaimah reveals the rugged beauty of these famed 'Fjords of Arabia'. Visit Telegraph Island (you can hire a boat cheaply from the port at Khasab) for a secluded swim in crystalline waters. The area is utterly unspoilt, with few tourists, so see it now before it gets discovered. Stop off for a drink at the Golden Tulip Hotel, take in the majestic views from top of Jebel Harim Mountain and have a total switch-off from Dubai's go-go pace.

Sharjah
This tiny emirate only 40 minutes from Dubai has been appointed a UNESCO centre of Arabic culture and heritage. With 15 museums, galleries, workshops and heritage sights like the 1820 Al Hosn Fort, Sharjah offers genuine insights into the local culture. It's much more conservative than Dubai however – no alcohol is served, and tank tops and shorts will cause offence. Wandering about Sharjah's souks and alleys, you could be in a tale straight out of 1,001 Nights.

Camel Polo

It had to happen sooner or later. Anyone wishing to try it out for themselves can call Dnata Travel on 04 404 5861 or email camelpolo@dnata.com.

Camel Racing

An authentic local sport, camel racing has been part of Bedouin culture for centuries. The races are atmospheric and exciting: robot jockeys (child labour laws now prohibit the former young riders) 'ride' the fleet-footed camels in thrilling, thundering contests that draw hundreds of fans. Keep an eye out for *souks* set up raceside with great bargains on things like decorative hand-stitched cotton camel blankets, which make attractive bedspreads. The times and locations vary so check with Dubai Tourism (www.dubaitourism.ae) or your hotel concierge.

Car & Go-Kart racing

Dubai Autodrome
Emirates Rd, Dubailand
Tel: 04 367 8700
www.dubaiautodrome.com

Dubai loves life in the fast lane and it doesn't get much faster than at Dubai Autodrome – the FI Association approved circuit. The 5.39km track is one of the most modern in the world; it is also one of the most challenging, with a combination of high-speed straights and technical corners. Take a spin in the Audi TT 2 litre Turbo, whose 2000cc engine gets you from 0-100 kms in 6.4 seconds. You can take lessons in high speed driving, or enjoy high-octane 330cc Go-Kart rides.

City & Desert Tours

Arabian Adventures

Emirates Holiday Building, Sheikh
Zayed Rd
Tel: 04 303 4888
www.arabian-adventures.com

A top operator on all levels, offering
a good range of city and desert tours.
Somewhat more expensive than other
companies, but worth it for their reliable service, high standards and indepth knowledge.

Big Bus Company

Tel: 04 324 4187
www.bigbus.co.uk

Air-conditioned double-decker buses
cruise around Dubai; running between
20 hop on and off stops at all the main
beach or city attractions and featuring
informative live commentary in English, often rather wittily. A great way to
get an overview of Dubai in a hassle-
free format, allowing you maximum
freedom to explore.

Desert Rangers

Dubai Garden Centre, Al Quoz
Tel: 04 340 2408
www.desertrangers.com

A one-stop source for action-packed
activities, this high-octane company
offers everything from mountain climbing to dune driving. Their overnight
desert safaris are highly recommended.

Gulf Ventures

Deira
Tel: 04 209 5568
www.gulfventures.org

One of the UAE's most reliable and
experienced tour operators with excellent local knowledge throughout the
region. Adventure touring particularly
good, with desert safaris and camping
in Oman, along with such activities as
polo, fishing, dune bashing and more.
They are very happy to help create itineraries and special tours depending on
your interests.

Creek Tours

Cruising the Creek is one of the 'must
do' attractions of Dubai for good reason. With the renaissance of this famous waterway has come spectacular
new buildings and a restored shoreline
featuring traditional homes of the early
traders, with their distinctive wind towers. The Creek defines Dubai much
the same way as the Thames in London or the Seine in France, playing a
major role in the city's economic development ever since Dubai flourished
as pearl fishing and trading village. To
take a cruise along the Creek is to see
the real Dubai in action, from ancient
dhows to the latest super yacht.

Bateaux Dubai

Downtown Bur Dubai
Tel: 04 399 4994
www.bateauxdubai.com

From its glass-enclosed interior, you
will be able to see a variety of Dubai's

most famous landmarks. Your journey begins just after sunset, as the first stars come out to compete with the twinkling lights of the city. As you float past Bur Dubai's wind towers, Deira's skyscrapers, and iconic architectural landmarks like the National Bank and the Dubai Creek Golf and Yacht Club, enjoy a four course à la carte meal, polished off with some excellent wines in a romantic, sophisticated setting (see EAT).

Tour Dubai
various locations
Tel: 04 336 8409
www.tour-dubai.com

Travel in a traditional Arabian *dhow* along the Creek for an hour tour with English recorded commentary about all the major landmarks. Private charters also available.

Wonderbus
Burjuman Shopping Mall
Tel: 04 359 5656
www.wonderbusdubai.com

Board the air-conditioned bus on land, and stay on as it plunges into the Creek for a two-hour amphibious adventure that takes in key sights along the Creek. Great fun for kids.

Extreme Sports

For the lowdown on everything you wouldn't want to try at home, from diving with sharks to leaping off cliffs visit www.adrenalinesportslive.com

Blue Banana
Business Central Towers
Dubai Media City
Tel: 04 436 8100
www.bluebananaarabia.com

One of the best sources for adrenaline-pumping activities in Dubai and the UAE. All you do is book and turn up, Blue Banana does the rest.

Golf

Dubai is a golfing mecca. Each year, the PGA Tour Desert Classic tournament brings gods of the game – Tiger Woods, Ernie Els, Vijay Singh and Nick Faldo – to the prestigious Emirates Golf Club. Other top golf clubs include the stylish Montgomerie, which boasts one of the world's longest 18th holes at 650 yards, the Four Seasons, with its modernist clubhouse, and the Dubai Creek Golf & Yacht Club, which benefits from a beautiful Creekside location. Your hotel can arrange a round at most of the courses, or you can book ahead at any course in the emirate using Dubai Golf's excellent reservations system. Call 04 390 3931 or visiting www.dubaigolf.com. All golf courses in Dubai are spikeless.

Arabian Ranches Golf Club

Dubailand
Tel: 04 366 3000
www.arabianranchesgolfdubai.com

Arabian Ranches is an 18-hole, desert style grass course, designed by Ian Baker-Finch in association with Nicklaus Design. It's a beautiful course, with a natural flow of the holes through the sand dunes and wonderful desert landscape. Miss the fairways and greens and you enter the 'sandy waste', with its indigenous shrubs and bushes. All standards of golfer will appreciate the GPS (Global Positioning System) yardage service available on every golf cart, and there are pros on hand for lessons. The Spanish Colonial style clubhouse features Ranches Restaurant and Bar, with a terrace overlooking the 9th and 18th holes. There is overnight accommodation available, with views overlooking the course or the lake. Step out of your room, hop onto your golf cart and it's off to the first tee.

Dubai Creek Golf and Yacht Club

Al Garhoud, Deira
Tel: 04 295 6000 www.dubaigolf.com

Located in a dramatic setting on the Creek and incorporating a yacht club and leisure centre, this, exceptional, recently refurbished club has a championship 18-hole, an impressive 6,839 yards in length. Three ornamental lakes and a three seawater hazards feature on the course. Designed in the shape of the billowing sails of a traditional Arabian *dhow*, the 45-metre high clubhouse captures the essence of Dubai's seafaring traditions and has spectacular views of the Creek. Golf goes on past sunset at Dubai Creek as the par 3 course, driving range and practice facilities are all floodlit to allow play late into the night. Visitors are welcome on a 'pay-as-you-play' basis.

Emirates Golf Club

Emirates Hills,
off Sheikh Zayed Rd
Tel: 04 347 3222 www.dubaigolf.com

Named among the world's top 100 golf courses by Golf Digest, Emirates Golf Club is Dubai's most famous golfing venue and the host of the PGA Tour. It sports two 18-hole championship courses: one, the Majlis, is the home of world-class events like the Dubai Desert Classic, and the second, Faldo, newly re-designed by golf legend and six-time major winner Nick Faldo. There's also a friendly yet testing 9-hole par-3 course, the Emirates Golf Academy, numerous practice facilities and two driving ranges. Leisure facilities include swimming pools squash and tennis courts, gymnasium, grass football pitches, and a well-stocked Pro Shop.

The Els Club

Dubai Sports City, Emirates Rd
Tel: 04 425 1010
www.elsclubdubai.com

Another exciting new championship course is The Dunes at the Els Club. Designed by golfing legend Ernie Els, the 18-hole, links-style course comprises 7,538 yards of neatly manicured Bermuda grass whilst five sets of tees, generous fairways and over 80 bunkers make it playable for all standards.

The Four Seasons Golf Club

Festival City
Tel: 04 601 0101
www.fourseasons.com/dubaigolf

Recently opened and already earning plaudits for its Al Badia course, designed by Robert Trent Jones, and stunning clubhouse. The club boasts a world-class academy showcasing the region's only TaylorMade Performance Lab and MATT swing analysis system, one of only six in the world. It has all the luxury you'd expect from the Four Seasons, with spacious, stylish locker rooms, Jacuzzi and sauna, steam room, rain showers and lounge areas. The Blades restaurant serves delicious Asian fusion cuisine in a dramatic setting overlooking the course.

The Montgomerie

Emirates Hills
Tel: 04 390 5600
www.themontgomerie.com

This award-winning golf resort is one of the Middle East's most luxurious. The championship course was designed by Colin Montgomerie in association with Desmond Muirhead and covers 265 acres that consist of 123 acres of turf, 49 acres of man-made lakes (a total of 14), 93 acres of landscaped gardens and is scattered with 81 large bunkers to provide an undulating links style golf experience. It is probably most famous for its 656 yard 18th hole. There's also a floodlit 9-hole

par 3 academy course, driving range, putting greens and Troon Golf Coaching. After-golf pleasures include treatments at the Angsana Spa, dining at Nineteen, and staying in of the most attractive, expensive golf resorts ($24 million was spent on the clubhouse alone) in the region.

The Tiger Woods

Dubailand
www.tigerwoodsdubai.com

The Tiger Woods Dubai is the first Tiger Woods-designed golf course and golf resort in the world. The planned golf resort will feature Al Ruwaya, a 18-hole golf course, state-of-the-art 60,000 sq ft clubhouse, golf academy, boutique hotel and residential properties. Dubai's golfing community are eagerly awaiting what is tipped to be one of the most exciting new golf resorts in the world.

Horse Racing

Dubai's fabulous racing scene is not to be missed. The season lasts from November to March. For details call the Dubai Racing Cub on 04 332 2277 or visit www.dubairacingclub.com

Horse Riding & Polo

For centuries, horses have been an integral part of the Arab world, symbols of wealth, status and position; admired for their beauty, endurance and speed. Dubai is an equestrian paradise, thanks to the horse-loving Al Maktoum family whose own Godolphin stables have won many awards and whose thoroughbreds grace racetracks around the world. The Arabian love of good horsemanship means there are plenty of chances to ride or play polo.

Dubai Polo and Equestrian Club
Arabian Ranches, Emirates Rd
Tel: 04 361 8111
www.poloclubdubai.com

Learn to play the 'sport of kings' at this excellent new venue, also offering stable tours and two-hour desert hacks in the early morning and late afternoon. The Dubai Polo and Equestrian Club has a unique Spanish hacienda-styled clubhouse, where guests and members can dine at Palermo, a steakhouse and grill restaurant, or enjoy tapas at the Argentinean themed Ippos Lounge. Other facilities include the Angsana Spa, where guests can indulge in exotic body wraps, soothing massages, hydrotherapy sessions and other treatments, as well as a large and well-equipped gym, outdoor swimming pool and sun-deck area.

Al Awadi Stables
Ras Al Khaimah
Tel: 05 09656870

Set within eight acres of landscaped gardens and paddocks, this friendly, unpretentious stable is a favourite among Dubai's horsey set. Rides, lessons and even camping are all available. Best in winter months as it gets extremely hot from March to October.

Jebel Ali Equestrian Club
Jebel Ali
Tel: 04 884 5566
jaridingclub@yahoo.com

Experienced riders can go for hacks along the beach or inland, and there are lessons available for all levels. Children welcome.

Microlight flying, paragliding, powered parachuting

Micro Aviation Club
Umm Al Quwain Airport
Tel: 050 350 4289
www.microaviation.org

Microlight flying is an adrenaline addict's dream. New fixed-wing microlights can dive 250 feet in a few seconds and zip through the air at a lightening quick 150 mph, although the usual cruising speed for sightseeing is 40 to 60 mph. Along with their amazing airborne sightseeing tours, The Micro Aviation Club runs classes on piloting a microlight as well as offering adventure trips to the Empty Quarter and Oman. Its fearless Hungarian founder, Laszlo Toth, is a Dubai legend.

Skiing

Ski Dubai
Mall of the Emirates, Jumeirah
Tel: 04 409 4000 www.skidxb.com
Open: daily, 10am–midnight

play...

Ski Dubai is a top attraction, and Dubai at its most surreal. In the middle of the desert, it's the world's largest indoor ski resort, complete with real snow, chairlifts, black runs, alpine chalets and burkha-clad ski bunnies grabbing air off a 90m quarter pipe. An hour Discovery lesson costs from Dhs140, including all the kit except hat and gloves. Open 10am to midnight.

Skydiving, skydive boogies, paramotoring

Umm Al Quwain Aeroclub
Umm Al Quwain Airport
Tel: +971 4 768 1447
www.uaqaeroclub.com

Highly professional, experienced team. Lessons and jumps available. A tandem jump with an instructor requires no previous experience although you will need to go through a safety orientation, and costs from Dhs 1,000.

Spas

Amara
Park Hyatt Hotel, Deira
Tel: 04 602 1234
www.dubai.park.hyatt.com

With a place on Condé Nast Traveller's Hot List and a waiting list for treatments, Amara is one of Dubai's favourite spas. Inspired by ancient Moorish palaces, the white exterior and royal blue domes of Amara, situated in front of an outdoor pool fringed with palm trees, offer a welcoming entrance into this secluded spa. The spacious, beautifully-appointed spa suites include a pretty outdoor garden relaxation area and rain showers. The new 'Jewels of Arabia' spa menu is based on the healing properties of precious stones: The spa gets very busy at weekends so to avoid disappointment, book ahead.

Assawan Spa & Health Club
Burj Al Arab, Jumeirah
Tel: 04 301 7777 www.jumeirah.com

Walking into the spa is like entering a jewel box. All the surfaces glitter and shine with semi-precious stone inlay, mosaics, gold leaf and sumptuous fabrics. There are sixteen luxurious treatments rooms, as well as steam, sauna, Jacuzzi and the prettiest indoor pool in Dubai, with a floor-to-ceiling window overlooking the Arabian Gulf. The separate ladies area has its own infinity pool and spacious, beautifully-appointed dressing room. The spa features La Prairie, Aromatherapy Associates and E'Spa products. The Health Club has all the latest Technogym and Kinesis equipment, with personal trainers on hand for coaching. As you'd expect from the glamorous Burj Al Arab, everything is done to the highest standard, with prices to match.

Cleopatra's Spa & Health Centre
Wafi City
Tel: 04 324 7700 www.waficity.com

Bustling, popular day spa located in the chic Wafi shopping mall with a vast array of treatments at prices lower than the five-star hotel spas. There's a wet area with a Jacuzzi, plunge pool, steam room and sauna, as well as an attractive *majlis* relaxation room. If you book a spa package you receive complimentary access to the outdoor pool area at the Pharoah's Club. Highlights of the spa include the Elemis signature facials, *rasul*, a Middle Eastern cleansing ritual using steam to open the pores and mineral rich mud to de-toxify, *ayurveda*, the ancient Indian health system using medicated oil based massages, and the signature Javanese Royal Treatment.

Givenchy Spa & Oriental Hammam

One&Only Royal Mirage, Al Sufouh
Tel: 04 399 9999
www.oneandonlyresorts.com

The sublime setting in an Arabian pavilion is the precursor to an exceptional spa experience. The Givenchy spa is for European beauty treatments and signature body massages like the Canyon Love Stone Therapy, while the gorgeous oriental *hammam* replicates the traditional Turkish bath. The full treatment lasts about an hour, consisting of steaming, bathing, being scrubbed with Turkish black soap and finally being massaged on a heated marble table. The result is super-soft, glowing skin and a de-stressed body.

Retreat

Grosvenor House, Dubai Marina
Tel: 04 317 6611
www.grosvenorhouse_dubai.com

Taking up an entire floor, Retreat has everything for top-to-toe pampering. Guests can choose from a range of treatments and sessions, from a dip in the outdoor terrace pool to a workout in the gym, or time in the Hydro pool – all within the privacy of the spa complex. The spa's signature treatment is the *rasul*, and men will enjoy 1847, a male grooming salon with the best shaves in town. Along with the fitness centre and spa, you'll find Jetset, a cool hair salon known for its retro chic and brilliant blow-dries, and N-Bar, for the ultimate mani- and pedicures

SensAsia

The Village, Jumeirah
Tel: 04 349 8850
www.sensasiaspas.com

A hip day spa with an oriental vibe, popular with Jumeirah's yummy mummies, who arrive in droves for the innovative massage treatments like the 'Morning After' to recover from the stress of all those parties. With clever add-on selections so you can tailor your own treatments, it's a fun alternative to the usual hotel spa.

Talise Spa

Madinat Jumeirah, Jumeirah
Tel: 04 366 6818 www.jumeirah.com

This award-winning spa is one of the biggest in Dubai, with separate men's and women's wings, and set in a lovely rambling garden featuring fountains connected by a waterway. There are 26 specially designed treatment rooms offering total privacy and comfort in a serene setting. Talise has an impressive range of holistic treatments, like the Crystal Facial, and features all-natural products from Sodashi. Facilities include steam rooms, sauna, plunge pools, relaxation area, a boutique brimming with tempting spa products and Magnolia, a delightful vegetarian restaurant with much of its produce grown in the gardens. Service is caring and professional. One of Dubai's most respected spas, and deservedly so.

The Spa
The Palace, Downtown Burj Dubai
Tel: 04 428 7805
www.thepalace-dubai.com

This new and beautiful spa radiates tranquillity. Its refreshingly straightforward spa menu includes a thoughtful and original selection of treatments, like the Hot and Cool Aventurine Stone Therapy and Moroccan Hammam, and the choice of pre-programmed soothing iPod music during your visit and luxurious Carita and Decleor products all create a pleasurable and truly relaxing experience.

Other excellent spas include the new **Spa at Atlantis**, with its fabulous boutique, huge range of products and choice of treatments, the peaceful **Timeless Spa** desert retreat at Al Maha, the trendy **Lime Spa** at Desert Palm and the Asian-inspired **Amrita**

Spa at Raffles. Whatever you choose for your Dubai spa escape, know that Dubai can be an oasis of well-being.

Water parks

When the heat starts to hit, cool off at Dubai's world-class water parks.

Aquaventure
Atlantis The Palm, Jumeirah
Tel: 04 426 1000 or 04 367 2001
www.atlantisthepalm.com

Big, beautifully landscaped and dominated by its landmark 27 metre-high Ziggurat, this aquatic adventure park has been a sensation since it recently opened. Highlights include the region's fastest free fall slide, which propels visitors through the shark-filled lagoon though a submerged transparent tunnel. One of the top water parks anywhere, Aqauventure has exciting kiddie play areas, a private 700 metre sandy beach, 2 km lazy river and plenty of white-knuckle rides. Located at the end of The Palm, it takes at least 40 minutes from downtown Dubai (longer during rush hour) but the soon to be opened monorail should make the journey faster. Admission is free if you are staying at Atlantis, otherwise expect to pay from Dhs190.

Wild Wadi
Jumeirah
Tel: 04 348 4444 www.jumeirah.com

Smaller, cheaper and more centrally-located than its huge new rival Atlantis, Wild Wadi is fun, friendly and perfect if you don't want to spend an entire day in the tubes – as you can happily play on all the rides and the lazy river in half a day. Highlights include the 'Jumeirah Sceirah' high-speed drop slide and wave flow rider for surf's up action. Admission is free for guests at Jumeirah resorts, otherwise admission is from Dhs165.

Watersports

Dubai has a huge selection of watersports available. Call the Dubai Watersports Association for details on 04 324 1031 or visit www.dwsa.net. Another option is to visit www.bluebananaarabia.com for a wide range of water-based activities, from powerboat tours to snorkelling excursions. Dubai Marina and all the main beach resorts have extensive watersports facilities. Among the best are the Jumeirah Beach Hotel, Madinat Jumeirah, One&Only Royal Mirage and The Ritz-Carlton.

Diving

With its warm, clear waters, abundant tropical fish and many dive centres, Dubai is a great place to get your PADI certificate.

The Pavilion Dive Centre
Jumeirah Beach Hotel,
Jumeirah
Tel: 04 406 8827
www.thepaviliondivecentre.com

This centrally located PADI Gold Palm IDC centre is one of the best in Dubai for visitors, with an excellent range of PADI courses for all ages and abilities,

including open water excursions for experienced divers.

Yacht charters

Do as the locals do – cool off in style with a group of friends and charter a boat for a day of fishing, snorkelling, swimming and cruising along the crystalline Gulf waters.

Bristol Middle East Yacht Solution
Dubai Marina
Tel 04 399 4994
www.bristol-holding.com

One of Dubai's leading companies for all manner of boat and yacht hire, from *dhows* to speedboats, and with packages to suit every budget. Fishing and water sport charters also available.

ENJOY Yachting,
various locations
Tel: o4 311 6568
www.UAEyachting.com

This innovative organisation offers a wide range of boating options throughout Dubai. There are scheduled outings as well as private charters. Sunset cruises and the powerboat taxi service (great for avoiding Dubai's traffic jams) are especially popular.

play....

Itineraries…

We've put together a couple of ideas for you if you have some time to spare and just want to get the best out of Dubai in the shortest possible time:

We've put together a couple of ideas for you if you have some time to spare and just want to get the best out of Dubai in the shortest possible time:

THREE HOURS
Head to **Bur Dubai**. Take a walk through the winding alleys of the textile souk behind the Dubai Museum, that lead to the creek and take a seat at **Beit Al Wakeel**, a cafe that hangs out over the water, for *shisha* and decent Arabic food. Then head for **Dubai Mall** where you can shop whilst being watched by sharks from the enormous and well-stocked aquarium. The view of the ever growing **Burj Dubai** (it is currently the tallest tower in the world, although not finished) is fabulous and you can ooh and aah over The Dubai Fountain in front of it (you guessed it, The World's Tallest Fountain).

A HALF DAY
Head to the **Gold Souk** in Deira. Even if you don't buy anything, you'll get a decent feel of old Dubai. And the 'your name in Arabic' gold necklaces make great souvenirs for friends. Grab an *abra* (boat) across the creek for pocket change and walk through the textile souk.
Lunch. For an authentic and old-school experience, go and bag a wipe clean table outside **Ravi's** in Satwa. This café is an institution and you won't get better Pakistani food in Dubai, or so all the taxi drivers say. Sheikh Mohammed is apparently a fan, although he gets his to go.

Follow lunch with a little shopping – this time head for the **Mall of Emirates**: The Dubai Mall may boast an aquarium, but if the heat is getting to you then a trip to this mall's indoor ski slope and snow park should be on your list. The Mall itself is one of the city's most popular, boasting all the big international brands. Warm up again with a fondue and a giggle at the inept skiers at bar/restaurant **Apres**.

A WHOLE DAY

Breakfast at **Lime Tree Café**, Jumeirah Beach Road. The Dubai version of the Sloane, the 'Jumeirah Jane' populates this café during the week. At the weekend, it's all young, pretty beachgoers (the sea is just across the road) tucking into the scrambled eggs and turkey bacon (not as disgusting as it sounds, trust me!).

Cross the road and take a look in pretty **The Village Mall** which has some of the best designer boutiques in the city, including multi-brand womenswear store S*uce and Ayesha Depala, one of the city's most popular home-grown designers. Grab a couple of amazing cupcakes from **Sugar Daddy's** to munch in the car as you head to **Souk Al Bahar** (ask the taxi to take you to the palace hotel – it's next door), opposite the Burj Dubai and the Dubai Mall, for a walk around the pretty fake *souk*. The best shop for souvenirs is 50C – their Sheikh Mohammed cushions are very cool for a little bit of autocrat interiors chic.

Lunch at the **Rivington** in the same **Souk**, where you'll get a great view of the fountain and the best fish and chips in Dubai. Walk over the bridge to the Dubai Mall, as above.

In the evening, head for drinks at the **Park Hyatt's Terrace Bar** with beautiful night-time views over the creek. Then head to Dinner at **Reflets par Pierre Gagnaire** – one of the most eye-popping gastronomic experiences in the city, especially if the Michelin man himself is around.

Then head downstairs to the Fairmont for the recently unbelievably OTT **Cavalli Club**, also in the Fairmont. A temple to the very-nearly-tasteless, the walls are dripping in crystals, the chairs are leopard and zebra print and everything from the crockery to the vodka is emblazoned with the raisin-faced designer's name. Finally, end up dancing at the **400 Club** – the queues attest to the fact that it still hasn't been knocked off its top spot by pretenders to the throne. Book a table to ensure smooth entrance.

play...

info...

Alcohol

Alcohol is served only in clubs, hotels, and hotel restaurants, plus a very small number of restaurant chains. You won't be able to get a drink at most restaurants, or buy alcohol at shops without a liquor license (only for expats), so stock up at the Dubai airport Duty-Free Alcohol can be very expensive, particularly wine and champagne. If you drive, please note there is zero tolerance for drink driving: you can be arrested if any alcohol is found in your system while driving.

Climate & Clothing

Dubai is mostly warm and sunny throughout the year, with slight rainfall in winter, and an average daytime temperature around 24°c. Summers are very hot and humid, with temperatures reaching 48°c. The best time to visit is from October to May. Pack light, as you will inevitably buy more than you think. Dressing by day, casual chic is the general rule and sunglasses are essential, while in the evening you can go for glamour. Dubaians are style-conscious, well-groomed and prone to glitz. Sloppy attire won't help you getting into Dubai's nightclubs. Lightweight summer clothing is suitable for most of the year, but pashminas or jackets are useful for the cooler evenings in winter and Dubai's arctic air-conditioning.

Dangers

Dubai is exceptionally safe, with an excellent police force and a law-abiding culture. As a result, going out at night is a real pleasure. That said, one should use common sense as you would in any city. Don't flash your cash, don't go home with strangers, don't get rides in unlicensed minicabs and keep your wits about you. Prostitution is on the rise and male visitors may get propositioned at a hotel bar or nightclub. Western women on their own may find that they are stared at, especially if wearing something a little revealing, but if you avoid eye contact or encouragement, any genuine harassment is very rare. On the public beaches if you are bothered by touts or flirts there is a hotline: 04 203 6398 for instant assistance. For emergencies dial 999.

Dialing codes

+971 is the international code for the UAE, Dubai's city code is 04. Mobile numbers in the UAE begin with 050.

Drugs

Make sure any prescription drugs are clearly marked as such. Unidentified pills have been known to be confiscated at Customs. Don't even think about bringing any recreational drugs, unless you feel like visiting one of Dubai's jails for a mandatory four years.

Geography

The second largest of the seven emirates that make up the United Arab Emirates, (UAE) and is located on the southern shore of the Arabian Gulf. It has an area of some 3,900sq km. Outside the city itself, the emirate is sparsely inhabited and is characterised by sand dunes and desert vegetation.

Getting around

Taxis – Dubai taxis are reliable, cheap and plentiful. The base charge is Dhs 3.50, or slightly higher if you call one, and then Dhs 1.60 per km. Hiring a driver for 12 hours costs Dhs 500 (£80). Most hotels will happily arrange a chauffeur driven car at reasonable rates. Car rentals are also available at the airport and through some tour operators, though you will need an international license and driving in Dubai is not for the faint-hearted. Most of the taxi drivers are from India or Pakistan and don't always have expert local knowledge, so be sure and have the exact address of your hotel. **Metro** – the eagerly awaited Dubai Metro is under construction, with the first two lines in Jumeirah due to finish sometime in 2009.

Abra water taxi – each *abra* carries about 20 people, with a charge of Dhs 1 per direct crossing per head, or Dhs 100 per hour for exclusive hire. "Rowing" *abras* are also available at 1 dirham per head or 30 dirhams per hour. *Abras* are available round the clock. **Walking –** Dubai was not designed with pedestrians in mind. What with the traffic, building sites and heat, walking outdoors here can be stressful, unless you are in one of the few pedestrian-friendly enclaves like Dubai Festival City, Dubai Marina, the souks or Bastikiya. Jaywalking is illegal and crossing Sheikh Zayed Road is dangerous unless you are at a proper crosswalk.

Getting There

Dubai's award-winning Emirates Airline(www.emirates.com) has the most flights from the UK to Dubai and has just launched the Airbus A380 Super Jumbo to Dubai, with such luxuries as showers and suites on board. British Airways and

Virgin Atlantic also offer frequent nonstop flights to Dubai. Dubai International Airport is about 30 minutes from the city centre. Taxis and buses can take you into the city, or hotels will arrange transfers. Taxis cost between Dhs 40–70.

Language
The official language is Arabic but English is Dubai's most spoken language.

Lost or Stolen Items
If you have anything valuable lost or stolen call the Dept for Tourist Security toll free: 800 4438.

Money
Currency is the Arab Emirate Dirham (AED), commonly known as dirhams (Dhs) – £1 = Dhs 5.3, $1 = Dhs 3.7, €1 = 4.8. ATMs are available throughout the city at and credit cards are widely accepted except in the souks and local markets.

Opening Hours
The UAE weekend lasts from Thursday afternoon to Saturday. During the week shopping hours are generally from 9am to 1pm, then 4pm to 9pm in the souks and traditional markets – however, in the shopping malls the shops are open throughout the afternoon. Most shopping centres are open from 10am to 10pm or later. On Friday, the Muslim holy day, most shopping centres open around noon and close early in the evening. During Ramadan shops tend to open later in the day and stay open later in the evening.

Ramadan
The Muslim holy month of fasting is a special time in Dubai but for tourists it can prove restrictive, so if you want to party hard it's best to check when Ramadan falls (it changes every year according to the lunar calendar). Muslims fast from dawn to dusk during this time, and few restaurants are open except at hotels. You should avoid eating or drinking in public before sunset. Nightlife is toned down, live music and dancing is not allowed and many clubs close for the month.

Religion & Etiquette
Islam is the official religion of the UAE, and 76% of its residents are Muslims. Compared to neighbouring countries, the UAE has a relaxed dress code: at the pool or on the beaches, swimsuits and bikinis are quite acceptable (but no top-

less bathing). Avoid revealing outfits in public, men should avoid wearing shorts. You should not photograph local women without their permission. Men can shake hands with other men, but men should not take a woman's hand unless she first offers hers. Avoid public displays of affection: a British couple found in flagrante on the beach was recently arrested.

Shopping

Dubai's duty-free status and incredible range of shops makes it one of world's great shopping destinations. In the malls the prices are set. In the souks and markets haggling is expected so don't be shy and make sure you get at least 25%-50% off the original price.

Time

The UAE is 4 hours ahead of GMT.

Tipping

Dubai is renowned for its excellent service and tipping is appreciated. 10% is standard. Hotel room rates are subject to a 10% service charge and a 10% government tax: check if these are included in the hotel rate before you book.

Useful websites

Dubai Department of Tourism and Marketing (DTCM) **www.dubaitourism.com** – the official site of the tourism office, full of useful information covering all aspects of Dubai. For comprehensive coverage of gigs and live music try Time Out Dubai **www.timeoutdubai.com**. Dubai's ruler, Sheikh Mohammad, has his own website: **www.sheikhmohammed.com**. If travelling with kids visit www.dubai-kidz.biz for the latest fun activities. For the latest Dubai news visit **www.godubai.com** or for current events **www.dubaicityguide.com**.

Water

Dubai's water is perfectly safe to drink, so don't feel you have to spend a small fortune on bottled water at your hotel.

index...